W9-BQZ-745

HOW TO

WORK WITH THE ONE YOU LOVE

AND LIVE TO

TELL ABOUT IT

HOW TO

WORK WITH THE ONE YOU LOVE

AND LIVE TO

TELL ABOUT IT

CAMERON AND DONNA PARTOW

BETHANY HOUSE PUBLISHERS
MINNEAPOLIS, MINNESOTA 55438

Published by Bethany House Publishers
A Ministry of Bethany Fellowship, Inc.
11300 Hampshire Avenue South
Minneapolis, Minnesota 55438

Printed in the United States of America.

Library of Congress Cataloging-in-Publication Data

Partow, Cameron.
    How to work with the one you love—and live to tell about it /
Cameron and Donna Partow.
        p.   cm.

    1. Couple-owned business enterprise.   2. Home-based
businesses.   3. Work and family.   4. Interpersonal relations.
I. Partow, Donna.   II. Title.
HD62.27.P37   1995
658'.041—dc20   95–20784
ISBN 1–55661–532–9   CIP

This book is dedicated to our daughter, Leah.
You are the reason we work together.

CAMERON AND DONNA PARTOW work together in their family business, Partow Communications. They enjoy traveling as a family to offer workshops on professional and spiritual growth. Donna is the author of *No More Lone Ranger Moms* and *Homemade Business* and a popular guest on more than 100 radio and TV talk shows. They make their home in Arizona.

Acknowledgments

Special thanks to:

1. Jerry and Mariette Holland, who modeled all that is best about husbands and wives working together.

2. Dave Podgor of Podgor Design Associates. Larry Wright, formerly of Prudential Home Mortgage, Pam Green of Melitta Coffee, and Ruth Ann Pepple of Genesis Realty Network. You didn't let the miles stand in the way of our business relationship. You are more than customers, you are *friends*.

3. Jill Dueck, faithful mother's helper, as dependable as the Arizona sun.

4. The many couples who participated in our research. Your insights and contributions were invaluable. Extra special thanks to those who allowed their stories to be shared on the pages of this book, including: Sue Ellen Allen and David Fraser; Bill and Diane Black; Howard and Jacki Bowers; Woody and Dayna Brohm; Susan and Barry Brooks; Reg and Eleonore Forder; Andrea Gold and Gary Yamamoto; Rex and Mary Ellen Griswold; Greg and Sono Harris; Perry and Gail Hayden; Jim and Jill Mapstead; Paolo and Margo Pignetelli; Jim and Naomi Rhode; Gera and Jim Witte.

Contents

Part Four
Managing the Business

Part Five
Family Matters

Introduction

By Cameron

When Donna and I decided to join forces in a family business, we had many obstacles to overcome. However, marketing, budgeting, and finances were not our problem areas. Rather, we had difficulty setting priorities, dividing responsibilities, and demonstrating plain old mutual respect. In other words, our biggest problem was learning how to work together! Today, even in the corporate world, more and more companies are recognizing the importance of employees having good relationships in the workplace. They have discovered that productivity and quality of work are directly affected by the quality of the relationships between co-workers. Many companies conduct life-skills seminars to teach their employees how to get along with one another. They offer courses in the four basic temperaments and circulate materials describing the ideal employee and the model manager in an attempt to promote better understanding of one another and to enhance relationships.

Unfortunately, when family members work together, they often don't see the necessity of also working on their relationships with one another. Pulling in different directions can be detrimental to both the business and to the marriage; whereas, pulling together can produce results beyond your imagination.

In our particular case, Donna started the business and I joined her several years later. I now work with her on a part-time basis, while still holding down a corporate nine-to-five job. Because our business is based on Donna's writing and speaking skills, she is the boss. (We'll have a lot more to say about this tricky issue in the chapter entitled "When HE's Joining the Firm.") Usually, it is difficult for a man to play second fiddle to his wife, especially when it comes to matters of business and bread-winning. I, too, had trouble with these issues. Eventually, however, I realized I needed to deal with the reality of what was best for our business and for our family. Both Donna and I knew that her business could not succeed without my management skills. We also knew that I could not launch a business without her entrepreneurial savvy. To be successful, we needed each other.

When we first moved to Arizona, I was unemployed for nearly a year. During this period, I learned several difficult lessons. I came to realize we couldn't depend on a corporation as our only source of income, because in today's economy, there's simply no such thing as job security. I saw the extreme competitiveness of the job market. I discovered companies were demanding more and more from prospective employees, while offering less and less in return. I experienced firsthand how easily self-image and confidence become tied to a job, and then how quickly they disappear when the job is lost.

These lessons prompted me to consider alternative ways of earning a living. Gradually, I came to realize how fortunate I was that my wife had already started a business, thus paving our way. Rather than resenting her unique skills and talents, I learned to be grateful for them, because they became the base of our business. We have discovered that more and more couples are beginning to look within their own ranks to build a secure future for themselves and their children. Each family member has a unique set of skills, interests, and experience he or she can bring to the enterprise. That's the way it was for us, and I believe it will be for you as well.

I sincerely hope as you and your family strive to achieve the New American Dream of having your own successful business that this book will serve as a guide and will make your journey a happier one.

By Donna

Imagine a husband and wife working side by side in complete harmony. Imagine a husband and wife at the helm of a wildly successful business. Imagine a husband and wife who travel at will, vacationing for a month at a time. Imagine the freedom of attending your daughter's afternoon ballet recital or your son's baseball game. Imagine taking the family to Disneyland—without asking the boss for permission. Imagine a couple whose respect for each other deepens with each passing day. Now, savor that picture in your imagination, and then get ready for a trip to reality.

Remember when the two of you decided to wallpaper? Oh, come on, every couple tries it at least once. And if you haven't, pick a room and get to work. It will give you an excellent idea of what working with the one you love is *really* like. Before we were married, I worked as a nanny for Mr. and Mrs. Incredibly Mellow. He was a brilliant seminary professor and she was an artist/ homemaker. I'm telling you, you've never seen a more harmonious couple—until that fateful day they decided to wallpaper the nursery. (Modern science still has not identified what compels expectant parents to do this; it is, however, an almost universal instinct.)

Well, this book isn't really about wallpapering—unless, of course, you actually *like* to wallpaper, in which case I recommend launching a wallpapering business that targets expectant parents! Nevertheless, wallpapering is an accurate metaphor for working together. It seems easy, it seems blissful, it seems romantic. In reality, it is hard, it is frustrating, and it is anything but romantic. At times, it will bring out the worst in you. However, eventually the two of you will discover a rhythm that works. She soaks the paper; he hangs it. She smoothes the wrinkles on the bottom of the wall; he works the ladder territory. Together, you pray for wisdom and grace when you discover . . . *the seams*! If you persevere to the end, you will have created something beautiful to behold.

Working together as a husband and wife team can be the most wonderful experience of your marriage. But at times, it can be an absolute nightmare. We know, because we've experienced both ends of the spectrum. We've often joked that we'd never hire a divorce attorney . . . a hit man, maybe!

The first time we tried to go into business together was a complete disaster. Cameron had been unemployed for months, while my business was booming. I realized I could generate more income if I could focus on writing and speaking and turn the routine side of the business over to Cameron. He agreed to give it a try and the battle was on.

Our marriage was already stressed to the limit because of Cameron's extended unemployment. His self-esteem had hit absolute rock bottom as he faced rejection day after day. I was feeling the pressure of being sole provider for our family. In addition, we had just moved from New Jersey to Arizona, where we had no family and no support network. To make life even more fun, we were basking in 110-degree heat, day in and day out.

We argued about everything. When Cameron didn't do things exactly when and how I thought they should be done, I became frustrated and critical. Cameron, in turn, insisted that I was being petty and overbearing. He also pointed out that I wasn't treating him like an equal partner; I was dumping all the junk work on his pile. In short, working together was driving us apart.

We are living testimony to the axiom: "Opposites attract, then they attack." Cameron, who was born in the Middle East, believes everything should be done properly and with absolute dignity. He never, ever raises his voice in public. He is constantly mindful of everything he does and would rather die than draw attention to himself. He considers politeness a top priority and carefully weighs every word he speaks, for fear he might inadvertently offend someone. As you might guess, he is liked by everyone. (I often quip that if a serial killer broke into our house and started attacking me, Cameron would advise me to keep my voice down so as not to disturb the neighbors! Besides, even a serial killer has feelings, and we wouldn't want to offend him!)

For all of you birth-order fans, I'm the youngest of eight children. And, yes, I'm the classic baby of the family. I will do anything, absolutely anything, to get attention. I say exactly what's on my mind and deal with the consequences later. Every day, I wake up with a new idea, a new cause, a new project to tackle. I am the Queen of Enthusiasm and love to shake things up and make things happen. More precisely, I like to start things. Finish things? Don't bore me with details. Even as I write these words, the floor of my home office is covered with piles of unfinished projects. I have a poster that says, "If you came to see *me*, Welcome! If you came to see my *house*, you'll need an appointment." Needless to say, I drive Cameron insane.

Our story is funny on paper, but in reality, it has often been painful. Like most couples, we've journeyed through our share of dark valleys. It's said that marriages are made in heaven, but we have sometimes wondered if our marriage was devised in a much hotter place. Yet, today, we are successfully working together. Today, we're actually *glad* that opposites attract. If Cameron were just like me and I were just like him, there's no way our business could succeed. Now, more than ever before in our fourteen years together, we truly need each other. Best of all, we have an exciting sense that our marriage really was made in heaven. It looks like God had a plan all along! Maybe He knew exactly what He was doing when He allowed two young people from opposites sides of the globe to cross paths, fall in love, and journey on together.

And, maybe, just maybe, you are part of the reason we came together. It is our hope and prayer that you will find strength, wisdom, and courage on the pages of this book as you seek to work together as husband and wife.

PART ONE

WORKING TOGETHER: IS IT FOR YOU?

1
An Emerging Trend ...
As Old as Time

HUSBANDS AND WIVES WORKING together is a hot new trend! In fact, it's the fastest-growing business category in America, up by a whopping ninety percent since 1980. There's no sign of a letup, either, now that the old American Dream of climbing to the top of the corporate ladder has been replaced by the New American Dream of business ownership. Many trend watchers predict that the current swell will become a tidal wave as more women hit the so-called "glass ceiling," and grow weary of trying to "have it all." They also project that thousands of men and women who fall victim to corporate restructuring will throw off the yoke of job security and will take the plunge into self-employment.

Greg and Sono Harris are a good example of America's new pioneers. Residing on nine acres of land in Oregon, they work together and they educate their five children at home. They have a dog and a cat, and eventually would like to own some livestock—a pony, some chickens, and maybe even a cow.

Meanwhile, Greg and Sono are capitalizing on the technology of the Information Age and are positioning their family business to succeed well into the twenty-first century. "We like to call it our compound," says Greg. "Our business is in a separate building across from our house and that's where our employees report to work. When I walk across the lot to my office, I make the mental shift from home to work. Yet I can be at the kitchen table for lunch within minutes."

Greg gets frustrated when he hears people say that a woman's place is in the home. He thinks *everyone's* place is in the home. Greg believes, as we do, that the Information Age will usher in the return of home and family as the center of American civilization. Already, nearly forty million Americans work at home and the number grows daily. Millions more have home computers, giving them access to the Information Superhighway from the comfort of their living room, den, loft, or what have you. True, not all couples who work together work at home, but a great many do. Many get their start at the kitchen table, later moving the business when it outgrows their home.

Before we explore the emerging "hot new trend" of husbands and wives working together, a little history lesson is in order. Prior to the Industrial Revolution of the 1800s, virtually everyone worked at home. Husbands and wives worked together to provide for the economic survival of their families. Not all were farmers; some were tradesman, shopkeepers, and professionals.

It wasn't until the emergence of the manufacturing plant, the assembly line, and the office building that men left home to work and the modern role of housewife was invented. (Note: We draw a sharp contrast between the stereotypical bored housewife of the 1950s and today's dynamic stay-at-home moms. For more information, see Donna's book, *No More Lone Ranger Moms*, Bethany House, 1994.) "In 1900, seventy percent of the American population was self-employed; only thirty percent relied on someone else to provide them with employment," notes Harris. "In 1980, those statistics were reversed. Only thirty percent of Americans were self-employed, while a whopping seventy percent were totally dependent upon someone else to provide for them and their families."

A broad range of factors is driving the current return of husbands and wives to home business enterprises. In addition to the fundamental shift from the Industrial Age into the Information Age, we have also seen the demise of job security. Both of us have experienced these changes in a personal and painful way; we suspect many of you have as well. As Greg Harris notes, "Today, job security is an oxymoron. It doesn't matter what promises the company makes, if the company gets bought out or circumstances change, all deals are off. That instability makes it very attractive for people to strike out on their own. Owning your own business is difficult, but at least it's a stable difficulty."

Rediscovering Family Values

Former Vice-President Dan Quayle stirred a firestorm of controversy during the 1992 Presidential Election with his "family values" speech. (He argued that children are better off if they live with both Mom and Dad, and if at least one parent actually works for a living. What a radical concept!) However, within a few years, people from both ends of the political spectrum were joining the chorus. There's simply no more denying that the American family is in trouble. No doubt we've all heard the widely quoted statistic that the average American father devotes twenty-seven seconds of his undivided attention to his children each day.

Yet, hope is on the horizon. A recent study conducted on behalf of the Hilton Hotels and published in the *Wall Street Journal* revealed that over eighty percent of Americans report their number one goal for the 1990s is to spend more time with their families. Daycare problems, burned-out supermoms, and shifting family priorities all play a role in the increased desire of many people—

especially women—to arrange their careers to allow more flexibility in caring for their families.

"There's a strong feeling among a lot of people," says Greg, "that if we don't do radical things to have a family, the next generation won't know what a family is. We sense that careerism is out of control, and we've realized that our children need to be included in all of our lives. That means our work lives as well as our recreational lives. Couples are looking for a strategy that gives them more freedom and control."

Business owners are among the few people who can really find that balance, because they have the time and the freedom to live according to their real priorities. That concept is appealing to more and more people every day. And that's why we believe the number of couples working together will skyrocket throughout the coming decade and into the twenty-first century.

What Successful Couples Do

Sharon Nelton, a reporter/writer for *Nation's Business*, interviewed sixty-three couples who successfully work together. In her book *In Love and In Business* (Wiley, 1986), she reveals nine key characteristics of successful marriage/business partnerships. We think it is absolutely remarkable how these characteristics reflect old-fashioned *family values*. Let's take a quick look:

1. Marriage and Children Come First.

Hmm-m-m-m. That doesn't sound like the power-grabbing, nothing-matters-but-my-career mentality preached during the 1980s. These successful couples discovered a wonderful truth: You don't have to sacrifice success for your family, and you certainly don't have to sacrifice your family for success. When you live according to right priorities, you enjoy greater success in every area of life. Part V of this book is devoted to "Family

Matters" including "What About Young Children?" and "Involving Your Children in Your Business."

2. Spouses Demonstrate Enormous Respect for Each Other.

Did you ever work with someone who thought the only way to get ahead was by putting everyone else down? Have you ever been guilty of acting that way yourself? If the put-down strategy is one of the skills you picked up in corporate America, now is the time to leave it behind. Successful entrepreneurial couples respect each other, and they go out of their way to demonstrate that respect in public. There is absolutely nothing whatsoever to be gained by putting down or otherwise disrespecting your mate. But there is much to be gained by praising him or her, publicly and loudly. Throughout this book, especially in Parts II and III, we will emphasize the importance of mutual respect. You'll want to take particular note of the chapters entitled, "Your Business Plan: Something to Point to . . . Other than Each Other," "When SHE's Joining the Firm," and "When HE's Joining the Firm."

3. High Degree of Close Communication.

Forget those interoffice memos and ninety-page reports that never actually said anything. Entrepreneurial couples enjoy a high degree of close communication. In fact, Nelton reports that these couples very often finish each other's sentences. They know what their partner is thinking. At the end of each chapter in our book, you'll find questions for reflection and discussion. Don't skip over these! They are designed to promote close communication. We'll deal specifically with improving communication in "Communication Skill-Builders."

4. Complement Each Other's Talents and Attitudes, and Carve Up Turf Accordingly.

Isn't it amazing how the very things that attracted you to your partner can sometimes drive you crazy?

When you read "Which Type of Partner Are You?" we promise you will fall in love all over again. You will gain a fresh appreciation for your differences and discover how important they are for insuring your business success.

5. *Supportive of Each Other.*

Since everyone has good days and bad days, one advantage of working together is that *one* of you is usually "up." When your other half is discouraged or has faced a major setback, it's your job as a friend and business partner to be supportive. We'll deal with the issue of providing practical support and encouragement in "Accountability Without Nagging or Dominating."

6. *Compete With the World Outside, Not With Each Other.*

We once listened to a husband and wife debating over who had the larger coffee table in his or her corporate office. These two competed with each other on everything. A small dose of competitiveness can actually be healthy, because it motivates both partners to ever higher achievement. Unfortunately, some couples let the competition get totally out of control. The person to beat is not the man or woman sleeping on the other side of the bed; it's the company doing business on the other side of town. Throughout this book, we stress cooperation rather than competition.

7. *Like to Laugh.*

We'll never forget the remark made by one woman we interviewed. She said, "My husband knows it's time to get me away from the office when I don't laugh anymore." Do you know research has revealed a direct correlation between humor and good health? If you haven't been laughing lately, maybe you're overdue for some fun! When you equip your business, don't forget to equip yourself with a healthy sense of humor. As Dwight

D. Eisenhower said, "A sense of humor is part of the art of leadership, of getting along with people, of getting things done."[1]

8. *Keep Their Egos in Check.*

Women, of course, have no difficulty with this because they are all so level-headed and modest. It's the men who get into ego trouble! (Just kidding, guys.) Egos can get in the way when business is booming *and* when business is bombing. When you get caught up in "How will that make me look?" rather than "What's got to be done?" you can make costly mistakes. When you start feeling invincible, you're equally vulnerable.

9. *Committed to Making Their Marriage Work.*

On those days when the grass looks greener on the other side, remember: if you lose the marriage, you lose everything. Nothing motivates like the "fear of total loss." And remember this, ladies, your husband may not be Robert Redford, but you're probably not Cindy Crawford, either. Besides, if Robert Redford were to come sweep you off your feet, you'd probably find out *he's* no Robert Redford, either! More than anything else, love is a decision. It's an emotion that grows or dies depending upon the emotional "food" we provide. Throughout this book, you'll find solid strategies for making your marriage work when you work together.

We've Got It Covered

Just think, by the time you've finished reading this book, you'll know exactly what it takes to work together successfully. Whether you already have a business and want to make it better or are just contemplating working with the one you love, you'll find the information

---

[1] "Quotes on Line" Software.

and motivation you need *right here*. From the nuts and bolts of business management to balancing your family and your business, we've got it covered. And so will you! So, let's get started.

For Reflection and Discussion

His Suitability Test

1. Are you committed to keeping your marriage and family top priority?

_____

_____

2. Do you demonstrate respect toward your spouse?

_____

_____

3. Do you feel your spouse respects you?

_____

_____

4. Do you enjoy close communication with your spouse?

_____

_____

5. Do you and your spouse have complementary talents and attitudes?

_____

_____

6. Are you willing to "carve up turf" accordingly?

_____

_____

7. Are you supportive of each other?

_____

_____

8. Do you enjoy strong family ties?

_____

_____

9. Do you view your spouse as a competitor? Or do you recognize that you must work together to compete with the outside world? (Be honest.)

_____

_____

10. Do you laugh often together?

_____

_____

11. Can you keep your ego in check?

_____

_____

12. Can your spouse keep her ego in check?

_____

_____

13. Are you totally committed to making your marriage work . . . even if it means giving up the business?

_____

_____

Her Suitability Test

1. Are you committed to keeping your marriage and family top priority?

2. Do you demonstrate respect toward your spouse?

3. Do you feel your spouse respects you?

4. Do you enjoy close communication with your spouse?

5. Do you and your spouse have complementary talents and attitudes?

6. Are you willing to "carve up turf" accordingly?

7. Are you supportive of each other?

8. Do you enjoy strong family ties?

_____

_____

9. Do you view your spouse as a competitor? Or do you recognize that you must work together to compete with the
   outside world? (Be honest.)

_____

_____

10. Do you laugh often together?

_____

_____

11. Can you keep your ego in check?

_____

_____

12. Can your spouse keep his ego in check?

_____

_____

13. Are you totally committed to making your marriage work
    . . . even if it means giving up the business?

_____

_____

2
What's the Appeal? The Advantages of Working Together

LIKE MANY MARRIED COUPLES, Susan and Barry Brooks often thought of taking their marriage partnership one step further and forming a business partnership. For several months, they tried to develop a brilliant business idea. What they wanted most of all, however, was a business they would both enjoy. One day in 1977, while sitting at their kitchen table, Susan asked, "What do we enjoy doing together?" Barry shouted, "Cookies!" Each year they had a blast baking holiday cookies, using old family recipes. Their cookie-filled tins were always a big hit with friends and colleagues.

Bankers, however, laughed at their plan. So the Brookses sold their home and used the proceeds to open a retail cookie shop. It became an instant success. By 1978, they had twelve franchises up and down the Southeast Coast. After encountering major problems with quality control, they decided to disassociate themselves from the company.

Starting over again, Susan and Barry moved to Tempe, Arizona. They still wanted to sell cookies, but not only through a retail store. "There were plenty of options, such as grocery stores, warehouse clubs, and gourmet shops. But we were looking for a unique niche," recalls Barry. That's when the second great idea hit. A friend of Susan's asked if the pair would bake cookies for her husband, a prominent surgeon, to give as holiday gifts to patients and colleagues. "Even as we talked, the idea began to click," recalls Susan. "Surely there were many professionals and executives who would like to give homemade cookies as gifts." Indeed there were.

Today, Cookies From Home sells eighty percent of its product to corporations and professionals. Each order is customized with the corporation's name and logo on the tin, packaging, and inner wrappings. For Valentine's Day, Psicor, a medical supply company in San Diego, California, placed an order for more than $25,000. "We packaged the cookies in Psicor's surgical containers and sent them to eight hundred of their customers. The customers were delighted to discover not needles and rubber gloves, but chocolate-chip cookies. The promotion was a huge success," adds Susan. The Brookses now have thirty employees, and projected sales for 1994 were $1.5 million.

Although Susan and Barry admit working together does have some pitfalls (see the next chapter), Susan insists, "The strengths far outweigh the hard times. My husband is the greatest partner I could dream of. He is always beside me, ready to forgive when I blow it. No matter what happens, I know he'll rally behind me and do whatever it takes to see this business succeed. He is my source of strength."

Having worked together for more than seventeen years, the Brookses have certainly had their share of dark times. Now that they've made it to the top, they are enjoying all the advantages of working together as husband and wife.

More Time Together

Remember when you and your spouse were engaged? No one else in the world existed but the two of you. You spent every possible moment together and could hardly bear to be apart. What happened? Well, many things.

Reality set in, for example, especially the reality of working in two separate worlds. If you both work outside the home, you're away from each other at least ten hours a day. You both pour a considerable amount of time, emotional energy, and creativity into your careers. Too often, you have little left for your spouse. This is particularly true for people who are in a career that does not suit them; it takes everything they've got to make it through the workday.

Often, though physically at home, you are mentally still back at the office. And fearing your spouse can't truly relate, you don't bother talking about your job frustrations. Problems are further exacerbated when one or both of you work in highly technical or specialized fields. Your job can become a significant barrier to conversation.

Couples with stay-at-home mothers may experience similar frustrations. He's off in an exciting world, generating cash flow and hobnobbing with the powerful and the beautiful. She's home changing diapers and battling over nap time. Such couples can begin to drift apart as they continue to journey down two very different paths.

When you work together, you join each other's daily life. You have something—actually, many things—in common. You have the same goals, the same plans, the same customers, the same products, the same co-workers. You have no shortage of things to talk about. In fact, your problem will be having too much in common to talk about. Many couples now living in separate worlds would love to have that kind of problem.

Enhances Mutual Respect

One day of working together left a permanent mark on the Partow marriage. We had spent eight weeks planning a full-day seminar on working at home. Donna was in charge of delivering the program, and Cameron was in charge of most everything else. By the end of the twelve-hour day, we collapsed on the couch, absolutely exhausted. Yet, we had to agree it was one of the most rewarding days we'd experienced in our married life.

Munching leftover chocolate chip cookies, we began to analyze why working together on the seminar had been such a joy, when our previous attempts to work together had been . . . well, downright miserable. We came up with some solid answers, which laid the foundation both for our new business venture and this book.

R-E-S-P-E-C-T was what we had experienced in a remarkably fulfilling way. It was the first time Cameron had ever seen Donna in action. Oh, he knew she could talk . . . and talk . . . and talk. He'd been listening to her talk for fourteen years. He thought her daily exuberance was merely annoying. Now he saw that her speaking could make a difference in people's lives.

Donna knew Cameron was organized and detail-oriented. (Oh my, how she knew that.) Yet, she always perceived his concern for perfection as a secret plot to drive her crazy. She knew he was gracious and hospitable, but always thought he was too much of a people-pleaser until she saw how much the seminar attendees appreciated all the little details he attended to.

Suddenly, Donna realized that Cameron could add a new dimension to the business that she alone couldn't achieve. She gained a new respect for his ability to deal effectively with people, for his ability to anticipate what was needed and provide it without being asked. Working together has dramatically enhanced our mutual respect. And it has dramatically enhanced our marriage.

Live by Your Own Values

Very few Americans have a greater opportunity to live by their own set of values than those fortunate enough to be self-employed. That opportunity was one of the things that attracted Bill and Diane Black (co-owners of Beyond Words, a five-year-old database management and publishing company) to business ownership. "We appreciate the freedom to get involved in organizations and causes we believe in," says Bill. "If we choose to volunteer for a day at our children's school or at our church, we have the flexibility to do so." The Big-Six accounting firm Bill formerly worked for would never have understood his desire to pitch in at church rather than at the office.

Set Your Own Hours

Now that you're the boss, you can take time off whenever you want to. Isn't that great? Of course, there is that minor little detail of generating cash flow! But did you know that lions work only four hours a day, yet manage to remain the King of the Jungle? That's because when they *do* work, they work with total concentration, total passion, total energy. They're the very best at what they do, maybe *because* they don't do too much of it. Working long hours is *not* the key to success; working smart *is*. In case you're wondering, lions usually sleep the other twenty hours each day. We think Donna may be a lion!

Couples who work at home have maximum flexibility. As Bill Black notes, "We have an almost unlimited amount of time to budget, however we see fit, according to the needs of the moment." Even storefront owners can exert control over their hours, although they must be prepared to accept the financial sacrifices that come with it. Rex and Mary Ellen Griswold, owners of Anzio Landing Italian Restaurant, close the restaurant every

Sunday and convert it into a church. It is attended by nearly five hundred people! Can you name many restaurant managers who are able to close the kitchen and open a church every Sunday?

Vacations and Mini-Vacations at Your Convenience

Okay, folks, throughout this book we will avoid being categorical, fanatical, or preachy. But we won't flex on this one, because it's too important. We noticed a definite *do* for couples who work together. Without exception, those couples who were *happily* working together (Not to be confused with those couples who were on the verge of killing each other. Yes, we did meet some of those.) took time out for vacations and mini-vacations. In some cases, they took a lot of time for vacation, even when they didn't really have the time.

The struggling couples insisted they never had time for vacations. It showed in their negative attitudes! More importantly, their businesses and marriages were clearly less successful. If you don't apply anything else you read on these pages, apply this one. Your mini-vacations do not have to be elaborate or expensive, but you do need to get away. Many couples take up outdoor hobbies like hiking or biking, which are inexpensive, yet re-invigorating. (Stay tuned for our new book, *The Active Family*, scheduled for release in 1996, by Bethany House.)

With a little advance planning and an attitude adjustment, you can turn business trips into mini-vacations. Rather than dreading business trips, you can look forward to them. "We often travel on business together, and we always have a great time," says Susan Brooks, co-owner of Cookies From Home. "We love to explore new cities, go to new restaurants and play the role of tourist. It keeps the excitement and romance of our marriage alive, especially when we're being pampered at a ritzy hotel."

Susan says she's a different person away from the office, and she has learned to depend on their business trips/mini-vacations to rejuvenate her. The Brookses used to have a second home in San Diego, where they would go one or two weekends per month. "We frequently had to travel to San Diego on business," explains Susan. "So it was convenient to get the work done during the latter half of the week, then stay over a couple of extra days for vacation. That second mortgage payment was about the best investment we ever made."

Susan estimates that she and Barry travel six times a year, spending about five days each time. "We go on sales trips or to trade shows, then we tack on a weekend just for fun. For example, last week we went to Los Angeles for six days. Two weeks before that we had a meeting in New York City. We worked during the day, but in the evening we went to the theater and had a blast."

In addition to their mini-vacations, the Brookses take an annual three-week vacation. "Last year, we spent three weeks hiking together in Italy," recalls Susan. "Another time, we went bicycling in Seattle for two and a half weeks. We enjoy active, physically demanding vacations, because we're forced to focus on what we're doing at the time, rather than on the work we left behind."

Howard and Jackie Bowers, owners of Bowers Travel, believe their vacations are an indispensable part of their business . . . and not just for the obvious reasons! Jackie says, "Hey, someone's got to check out all those fabulous resorts. We wouldn't want to steer our customers wrong." She adds, "We try to travel as often as we can. That's actually how we put the business away for a while. We do two spectacular vacations per year, in addition to frequent long weekends. We have traveled by hot air balloon, yacht, jet, and helicopter. We once landed by helicopter on the front lawn of a French chateau, then went inside and had a fabulous dinner."

For their long weekends, they have a place on the beach in California and a condominium at a ski resort in Utah. "We can get to either location within two hours. I can tell when Howard is in trouble; his answers are short and not well thought out. Then we know it's time to get away, for the sake of our business and our marriage. We get away twenty weekends out of the year."

(Important note to our readers: Please don't feel bad, we're insanely jealous of the Brookses and the Bowerses, too! Not many of us will ever be able to enjoy the incredible travel opportunities they do. However, we *do* have control over our time, so it's conceivable if we can come up with life's second most elusive quantity: money. There's always good old cheap camping!)

Common Purpose

For us, the greatest blessing of working together has been an incredible sense of common purpose. We know where we're going and we're pretty confident we'll make it! Of course there are details to work out and obstacles to overcome along the way. Nevertheless, our mission is clear; the path is mapped out before us, and we both know what we have to do to get there. Achieving our goals will require our pulling together, so there's no point in pulling apart or putting each other down. That's why we're always so sweet and loving twenty-four hours a day! And we also have a bridge for sale in the Everglades.

More Available for Your Children

When Donna decided to work at home back in 1988, her primary motivation was her bulging tummy. We were expecting our first child and Donna's top priority was to be an available mom. Many families, including ours, now recognize the importance of having an available father as well.

However, home-based parents are not the only ones who can be available to their children. For example, Suzanne Shell doesn't let running a storefront shop prevent her from remaining an available mom. She actually home-schools her thirteen-year-old son, Eric, at the upholstery shop she operates with her husband.

"Eric has his own desk and an old Commodore computer at the shop. He is set up in an area apart from customer traffic, so he can concentrate on his studies. The vast majority of our customers, when they see him helping out and discover we home-school, are very supportive and positive. This fall, my seven-year-old niece will be joining Eric as a home-schooler in the shop. My mother-in-law is French, so during lunch, she teaches all of us French and German language lessons."

Now, imagine taking your thirteen-year-old to your current job, setting him up with his own computer and explaining to all your co-workers that he is "going to school." Good luck!

We are also home-schooling our daughter, Leah. This works out well for us, because we travel as a family to conduct workshops around the country. For one thing, it keeps Donna's ego in check; Leah's fan club is usually significantly larger than hers. Recently, while Donna was autographing books and feeling very important, Cameron graciously pointed out that twice as many people were waiting in line for Leah's autograph. So much for being a pseudo-celebrity. If we were to put Leah in a traditional school, we'd either have to leave her behind, or we'd be constantly pulling her in and out of the classroom. We don't like either of those options. Besides, she is so charming and hilarious, we need her around for entertainment.

Ability to Involve Your Children in Your Business

In addition to attending school at the shop, Eric Shell has begun learning his parents' trade. "He takes all the old seat covers off of cars, boats, and trucks. He also removes interior trim pieces from cars and trucks, and removes old upholstery from furniture. In addition, Eric cleans up the shop and showroom floors, cleans the bathrooms, and dumps all garbage."

Suzanne reports, "Eric started out at one dollar per hour and is now up to two dollars per hour. He is just starting to install new covers on truck seats. When he learns to do it well, he'll get another raise. Of course, he's already announced that he does *not* want to be an upholsterer when he grows up. That's fine with us. He is learning how to run a business, how to interact with customers, and how to be responsible. Those skills will serve him well no matter what profession he chooses for himself."

A Legacy and an Inheritance

Greg Harris, director of Christian Life Workshops and owner of several business enterprises, believes strongly in leaving business ownership skills as a legacy and inheritance for our children. "I want to leave my children something other than a pile of cash. That doesn't mean we should expect our children to stay in the business forever, whether they like it or not. But at least they will inherit the skills and know-how to run their own business. Whether it's this business or another, they'll carry on the legacy of independence and self-employment. I want my children to know how to be the head and not the tail."

For Reflection and Discussion

Rank (from 1 to 10) how important each of the following advantages are to you.

Him   *Her*

____   ____   Having more time together

____   ____   Enhancing mutual respect

____   ____   Living by your own values

____   ____   Setting your own hours

____   ____   Taking vacations and mini-vacations

together

____   ____   Having a common purpose

____   ____   Being more available for your children

____   ____   Involving your children in your business

____   ____   Leaving a legacy and an inheritance

3
Guarding Against Potential Pitfalls

WORKING TOGETHER WITH the one you love, reaping advantages like they're going out of style—ah, does this sound like bliss? Better get prepared for a dose of reality as we consider the potential pitfalls, and more importantly, how to guard against them. The most valuable information in the world is SHK—secondhand knowledge. With SHK, you reap the benefits of others' hard-earned lessons without having to earn them yourself. So we're offering you the insights we have gained through our firsthand experience—and the firsthand experience of dozens of couples we interviewed.

One Income Source
(Can Be Devastating If Lost)

Time to roll out an old cliché: don't put all your eggs in one basket. No doubt your grandmother taught you that little ditty, and she was right to some extent. When you depend solely on the family business to bankroll the family, you're taking a risk. You have only one source of income and if you lose it, you lose everything.

If you want to reap the rewards—the advantages we talked about in the previous chapter—then you must assume some risk. We are referring to calculated risk, not reckless risk. The best way to guard against this particular pitfall is with a slow, steady approach. We strongly recommend that one spouse launch the business, while the other keeps his or her feet firmly planted in corporate America, the place where steady paychecks and health benefits flow.

Only when the business is firmly established—according to very clear guidelines covered in a later chapter—should the second spouse leave behind his or her corporate job. You won't find a surefire guarantee against business failure, but proceeding with caution is as close to one hundred percent safety as you'll get. Besides, the spouse who escapes will have *so much fun* tormenting the poor soul trapped on the corporate treadmill. We wouldn't want you to miss out on that!

All-Consuming Factor

This is, without question, the number one complaint of couples who work together. We heard it over and over and over. The business becomes like a weed in the garden of your marriage and you must constantly battle it back. The best advice we have heard came from Sue Ellen Allen, a professional speaker who works at home with her husband. "Make sure you both absolutely love what you're doing. That way, when it takes over your life—and believe me, it will—you'll be so happy you won't even notice."

Loss of Perspective on the Real World

Picture the two of you, hunkered down, battling the competition and fighting the good fight for economic survival. Now picture the two of you losing touch with the real world. It can and does happen. (Hint: When you don't have any friends left, because they can't bear to

42

hear you talking about the business anymore, you've lost perspective.) That's why it's so important to make a conscious effort to cultivate outside activities. You may want to take up gourmet cooking, enroll in an evening class, or buy a pair of bicycles.

Once again, let's not overlook the humor factor. Odds are, one of you will be really poor at some of the interests you pursue—and that will be tremendously amusing for your spouse! If you'd rather be nice to each other, join a hiking or camping club. It's pretty hard to mess up walking, and if neither of you knows the first thing about camping, you will provide hilarious entertainment for the people pitching tents around you. (You should see *us* trying!) More importantly, time spent in the great outdoors has a marvelous, almost miraculous, way of putting us back in touch with the big picture.

Loss of Company Benefits (Especially Health Insurance)

This is a big issue and we won't try to sugarcoat it. Health insurance is a major, major problem if you both devote full time to your business and it's not yet profitable enough for you to obtain good medical coverage. Again, we suggest that one partner remain in corporate America—and cling to those benefits—until your business is well established and you can afford to buy your own insurance.

No Company Pension or Retirement Plan

Here's another major disadvantage of making it on your own. The antidote is a heaping dose of self-discipline. First, self-discipline to conduct your business in such a way that it becomes profitable and wildly successful. Secondly, self-discipline to establish your own retirement plan and consistently contribute to it.

Stress on Marriage

Do we need to expound on this? When your business faces tough times, your marriage will face some tough times, too. Ironically, even when business is booming, some couples experience marital stress. Bill Black admits, "We expect more of each other, sometimes unfairly, than we would of an employee. Cutting the other person some slack is the hardest lesson we've had to learn. We know what the other person is capable of, and it is easy to demand it."

He and his wife, Diane, report experiencing stress because "we're constantly aware that if one doesn't hold up his or her end of the load, it puts more pressure on the other spouse. So we feel this incredible pressure to never slack off, to never take it easy for a minute."

Business Partnership Failure (and/or Marriage Failure)

Thousands of businesses fail every year. The failure rate is especially high for companies just starting up and for companies with substantial debt. In a later chapter we'll discuss why this is so and give steps you should take to prevent a business failure. Meanwhile, more than half of all American marriages end in divorce. As we've said before, when you lose one, you may well lose the other. Are you getting nervous yet?

On the bright side, "fear of total loss" is one of the most powerful forces known to humankind. Most couples who work together, therefore, feel far more motivated to succeed in both marriage and business. They put extra effort toward both fronts, for fear of losing either.

Loss of Passion in Your Marriage

As one woman pointed out, "Try to remember that you married your husband because you were in love

with him, not because he could do nifty spreadsheets."
When a husband and wife constantly talk shop, romantic conversation can be neglected.

Here again, many couples turn a potential pitfall into
a powerful force for good. Sensing the danger, they
make a conscious effort to continue "dating" each other.
We can't stress enough the importance of actively cul-
tivating the romantic side of your relationship. Husbands, if you won't romance your wife for the sake of
your marriage, do it for the sake of your business. Bring
her flowers, especially when it's not her birthday. Take
her out to dinner, especially when you can't afford it.

And wives, work hard to be attractive to your mate.
If your marriage, or your business, is in trouble, try arranging a romantic evening or weekend getaway with
your husband. Keep those marriage fires burning.

Resentment (If One Partner Wants to Withdraw or Pursue Another Opportunity)

You married each other for life, but did you marry
the business for life? Let's hope not. It is entirely possible that one spouse will want to withdraw from the
business, either to retire or to pursue other opportunities. Please, give each other room to grow and change.
Just as you welcomed your spouse into the business, be
willing to release him or her from the business when the
time comes.

Income Plateauing

Now that the average pay raise at most corporations
hovers around three percent, income plateauing for the
self-employed is not a big issue. Nevertheless, it is an
issue worth addressing. When you work for someone
else, you'll likely receive a raise once or twice a year. You
can pretty much bank on your income keeping pace

with inflation, provided you are a reasonably competent employee.

Business owners enjoy no such guarantees. We get a raise when the business increases in profitability. Unfortunately, when the business reaches a plateau, so does your income. On the positive side, of course, your *potential* income is theoretically unlimited. Unlike an employee, you have the right to a raise or a bonus whenever you want it. That's what being the boss is all about, right?

For Reflection and Discussion

Brainstorm three specific ways you will guard against each of the following potential pitfalls:

1. Dependence on one income._____

_____

_____

_____

2. All-consuming factor._____

_____

_____

_____

3. Loss of perspective on the real world._____

_____

_____

_____

4. Loss of company benefits._____

_____

_____

_____

5. No pension or retirement plan._____

_____

_____

_____

6. Stress on marriage._____

_____

_____

_____

7. Business partnership failure._____

_____

_____

_____

8. Loss of passion in your marriage._____

_____

_____

_____

9. Resentment (If one partner wants to withdraw or pursue other opportunities.)_____

_____

_____

_____

10. Income plateauing._____

_____

_____

_____

PART TWO

NUTS AND BOLTS

4
Choosing the Right Business

HOW CAN YOU CHOOSE the right business? If you and your spouse already have a business underway, how can you be sure you have chosen the right one? Even if your business is profitable, you may need to make a change if you: (1) are extremely unhappy working together, (2) have nagging doubts about whether or not you are in the right business, (3) are unsure if the business you plan to enter is really right, or (4) have no clue what you want to do.

Reg and Eleonore Forder provide a perfect example. They started a very profitable business, Century Vending, shortly after their marriage ten years ago. "We enjoyed working together, but we wanted more. We wanted something meaningful and fulfilling. We both had a passion for traveling, so we were constantly trying to think up something we could do that would allow us to travel," recalls Reg.

Seven years ago, the coordinator of a Christian writer's conference asked Reg if he would consider taking over the annual event. "I had attended the conference six years in a row and really enjoyed it. The woman said she wanted to retire, and felt I was the right person to continue her work. Eleonore and I discussed it and agreed to help. We had absolutely no idea it was going to become a full-time business for us. The first year, we lost $2,000 of our own money. But the response was great, so we did it again. The second year we lost only $1,000. It wasn't until the fourth year that we actually turned a profit."

So why did the Forders keep at it? "We didn't care at all about the money; we loved what we were doing. People would come to us during the conference and say, 'This has changed my life!' It was so much more rewarding than selling soda and snacks." Ironically, it was that soda and all those snacks that kept the writer's conferences afloat.

Reg and Eleonore were frequently hearing from aspiring Christian writers who wanted to know how to get started, or how to publish their work. Some just needed encouragement to persevere. As word of the conference spread, people began coming from out-of-state: California, Nevada, even Texas. "Several years ago, writers began asking us to bring the conference to their city. One writer's group from Dallas was especially persistent, but we kept turning them down, year after year. We told them we were just running this conference on the side, as a ministry. Last year, we finally gave up and said, 'Okay, we'll come to Dallas.' " The conference was a huge success.

As soon as the Forders returned from Dallas, they began pursuing the writer's conferences on a full-time basis. Meanwhile, Century Vending continued to chug along quite profitably. "We looked at every city in America with a population of two million or more. Then we targeted a dozen cities that didn't have a decent Christian writer's conference already."

In 1994, the Forders scheduled twelve conferences—one per month across the United States—plus a seven-day Caribbean Writer's Cruise.[1] Today, the Forders re-

---

[1] Donna attended the Forders' conference in Arizona, where she met Steve Laube of Bethany House Publishers. That meeting led to this book! If you want information on a writer's conference near you, call 1–800–21-WRITE.

ceive hundreds of calls each week from aspiring writers all over the country. They also bought *The Christian Communicator*, a magazine for writers and speakers. Within five months, they doubled their subscription base. "The magazine generates income and is the primary vehicle for promoting our conferences and the writing services we now provide." In addition to the phone calls, the Forders process approximately one hundred letters per day. Most contain orders for books, tapes, magazine subscriptions, and conference registrations. "Now we're looking to expand into book publishing, specializing in books for Christian writers," says Reg.

Thanks to the large volume, the Forders already rely on dozens of independent contractors and expect to hire their first employee in the near future. More to the point, they couldn't be happier. "It's absolutely everything we love to do," says Reg. The Forders are planning to sell their vending company. They bought a forty-foot, top-of-the-line motor home, complete with bedroom and home-office-to-go, from which they run the conferences. They now spend most of their time traveling around the country.

The Forders started a very successful business, but it wasn't really the *right* business. Rather than rest on their laurels, or settle for a life that was less than they dreamed of, they pressed on. They followed their passion, found a need, and filled it. The rest is rapidly falling into place.

Get Back in Touch With Your Dreams

In trying to determine the right business, we truly believe the most important question to be explored is this: What were your childhood dreams? The Bible says God "will give you the desires of your heart" (Psa. 37:4). We believe this means that God places within each of our hearts a vision for who we should become and what role we should fulfill. Unfortunately, the clamor of life often drowns out that still small voice. Your father wants you to be an attorney, your mother wants you to be an architect, your football coach thinks you have the potential to turn pro, and your favorite teacher longs to see you follow in her footsteps.

Pretty soon, you are living your life according to everyone else's wishes and expectations, and you have forgotten who you were created to be in the first place. Maybe you've spent ten, twenty, thirty years or more heading in the wrong direction. But it's never too late to change course. As you take the helm of your own company, you have an unparalleled opportunity to steer your life in a new direction.

Lest you think all this talk about childhood dreams is mere psycho-babble, consider this: A study was conducted in Britain of fifty children between the ages of seven and fourteen. The researchers asked the kids the immortal question: "What do you want to be when you grow up?" When they caught up with the participants thirty years later, those people who were pursuing their childhood dreams were more successful and more fulfilled than anyone else in the study.[2]

Yet, it is so easy to get sidetracked along the way. That's what happened to Donna. Here's her story:

All my life, I (Donna) dreamed of being a writer, although I had never met a writer until I was in college. My father was a truck driver, and my mother was a housewife. They were proud of my academic accomplishments, but they didn't exactly prod me on to become the next Annie Dillard. Yet, when I dreamed of the future, I envisioned myself sitting on the beach thinking great thoughts by day and writing beside a roaring fireplace by night.

Somehow I lost sight of that vision. Instead, I went

---

[2]Brian Tracy, "The Psychology of Achievement," audio cassette by Nightengale-Conant.

to college and then climbed aboard the corporate ladder. I worked absurd hours for dirt pay and for absolutely no recognition. In the end, I finally worked for an excellent boss, Robert Pollak, who believed in me and encouraged me to use my talents on the job. That happy arrangement lasted just long enough to give me the confidence I needed to strike out on my own, after the company was downsized. Thanks, Bob!

After losing $500 million in bad loans, the large bank I worked for laid off thousands of employees. My co-workers and I were given approximately one hour to clear out. I remember walking the streets of Philadelphia in a daze. The corporate ladder I had been climbing was suddenly kicked out from under me and I didn't know how I would ever get back on my feet again.

Eventually, I stopped blaming my employer and dealt with the situation as it was, not as I thought it should be. Looking back, I can honestly say that losing my job was not only one of the worst days of my life, but also one of the best. Why? Because it forced me out of my comfort zone. It put me back in touch with what I really wanted to do with my life.

If that bank hadn't tossed me off the corporate treadmill, I would still be sitting behind a desk in some stuffy office shuffling papers from pile A to pile B. I'd still have constant stomach trouble, commuting headaches, recurrent nightmares, frequent bouts with the flu, battle scars from office politics and other fallout from the corporate lifestyle. Worst of all, I'd still be living in an over-priced, overcrowded suburb of Philadelphia rather than in the beautiful high Sonoran desert of Arizona. *How can I ever thank the bank enough?*

Perhaps you've faced similar setbacks. Perhaps that's why you have decided to strike out on your own. Please believe us: There *is* life after corporate America. You *can* create a successful business with help from the one you love. And together, you can learn to make it on your own. The key is choosing a business that's right for both of you.

That's the first component of the Partow's Top-Secret Business Success Formula: Your Passion. Enthusiasm is the greatest asset in the world. It beats money and power and influence. Malcolm S. Forbes once said, "Your adrenaline has to run. Whatever business you're in, if you don't feel exhilarated by achieving your objectives and excelling in what you're doing, then you will never do very much well."[3] In the words of Ralph Waldo Emerson, "Nothing great was ever achieved without enthusiasm."[4] (We'll be revealing the other two components of business success in coming chapters. So keep reading) Just remember:

YOUR PASSION+ _____ + _____ =SUCCESS

Now, take a few moments to work through the Self-Evaluation Tool provided on the following pages. When you have completed your worksheets individually, come together and compare answers.

Her Self-Evaluation Tool

1. What do people COMPLIMENT you about? Can you parlay those talents or personal traits into a business?

_____

_____

_____

2. What ENERGIZES you? A business that excites you is a sure winner.

_____

_____

---

[3]Quotes on Line: "Words from the Wise," by Keith D. Mohler, AskSam Software, 1992.
[4]Ibid.

3. What do you enjoy READING? What section are you drawn to in the bookstore or library?

_____

_____

4. What do you enjoy doing with your FREE TIME? It is often said, "Do what you love and the success will take care of itself."

_____

_____

5. What PROBLEMS have you SOLVED around the house or on the job. Chances are other people have similar problems and will be glad to pay for your solutions.

_____

_____

6. How much TIME and MONEY can you invest? Some businesses require more of each than others. Choose wisely.

_____

_____

7. Based on the above, evaluate whether your current or planned business is really well suited to you. Indicate any modifications you might want to make.

_____

His Self-Evaluation Tool

1. What do people COMPLIMENT you about? Can you parlay those talents or personal traits into a business?

2. What ENERGIZES you? A business that excites you is a sure winner.

3. What do you enjoy READING? What section are you drawn to in the bookstore or library?

4. What do you enjoy doing with your FREE TIME? It is often said, "Do what you love and the success will take care of itself."

5. What PROBLEMS have you SOLVED around the house or on the job. Chances are other people have similar problems and will be glad to pay for your solutions.

_____

_____

_____

6. How much TIME and MONEY can you invest? Some businesses require more of each than others. Choose wisely.

_____

_____

_____

7. Based on the above, evaluate whether your current or planned business is really well-suited to you. Indicate any modifications you might want to make.

_____

_____

_____

Evaluating the Future Viability of Your Business

Once you've discovered the right business for your skills and interests, you are ready to consider the second component in our business success formula:

YOUR PASSION + FELT NEED + _____
=SUCCESS

In order to succeed, your business absolutely, positively *must* address a felt need in the marketplace. If it ain't broke, no one will pay you to fix it. Have you packaged your business for success? Is it *viable*? Webster defines *viable* as "capable of growing and developing." Does your business have genuine staying power? Following is a seven-point strategy for evaluating the success potential of any business idea. Even if your business is already underway, this exercise will provide clarity and direction for your venture.

The Viability Test

1. Are other people achieving similar OBJECTIVES with similar businesses? Check out the COMPETITION. Do you like what you see in terms of their lifestyle and the amount of money they are earning? Example: If you operate a daycare center and have dreams of becoming a millionaire, look around.

_____

_____

_____

2. Can it be HOME-BASED, at least initially? This will keep overhead costs down long enough for you to iron out any wrinkles. Example: You're interested in selling health food. Rather than opening a storefront from day one, start with a mail order business and establish your clientele before the Grand Opening. Indicate your strategy for working at home the first year.

_____

_____

_____

3. Do you have an existing CUSTOMER BASE? If not, do you at least travel in the right circles with people who are likely to need your product or service? Example: Everyone wants to market to lawyers. It seems like a great idea—after all, they've got the money. However, if you don't know any lawyers—and you don't know anyone who knows any lawyers—you're going to have a very tough time cracking the market. If, on the other hand,

your father, your brother, your sister-in-law, and five of your closest friends are all attorneys with prominent law firms, you've got a fighting chance. Just be realistic. List five people or five businesses who represent solid prospects; i.e., people you can call tomorrow and make headway toward closing the sale or engaging in serious networking.

_____

_____

_____

_____

4. Is the market FLOODED? A few years ago, gift baskets were listed among the hottest businesses to get into by *Entrepreneur Magazine*. Not anymore! Why not? Because hordes of people leaped into the arena looking to make a quick buck. As a result, the market became overcrowded and profits plunged. Here's a quick way to check whether or not your prospective market is flooded: Take out the yellow pages and see how many businesses already exist in the line you are considering. One hundred listings may be a very bad sign; i.e., there's no room for you to compete, at least not profitably. (Remember the Laws of Supply and Demand.) Note what you discover below.

_____

_____

5. Is the market READY? Zero listings in the yellow pages may also be a bad sign. If you come up with an idea that no one else has ever thought of, there's only one of two possibilities. It's either incredibly dumb or you've got a million-dollar bonanza on your hands. How

can you tell the difference between a winner and a hare-brained scheme? The winner addresses a compelling and far-reaching FELT NEED. (A felt need is a specific problem experienced by an identifiable group of people.)

Remember this: It's much easier to convince a potential customer to buy from you, rather than the competition, than it is to convince them they need the product or service *at all*. Is the market ready for your product or service?

---

6. Is there a SUFFICIENT market with GROWTH POTENTIAL? Conduct market research to insure enough companies or individuals need what you plan to offer. Here's a silly illustration. Let's say Bob and Sue Spider-lover feel passionately about tarantulas. From earliest childhood, they both dreamed of spiders. One problem: their pet tarantula, Fuzzy, keeps running away from home. It breaks their hearts. This is a serious problem. So they develop a solution: the tarantula leash. Sounds like a great business idea, right? They're building a business based on what they feel passionately about—that's good. They've solved a specific problem experienced by an identifiable group of people—also very good. They may even have developed a dynamite plan for financing, manufacturing, and distributing their tarantula leashes. What's missing from the equation? Thank heaven, there aren't enough lunatics with a burning desire to walk their pet tarantulas! Is there a sufficient market for *your* product or service?

---

7. Can you COMPETE? There are only three ways you can compete in the marketplace: better, faster, or cheaper. If you can do all three, you've got it made. Indicate on what basis you can compete or how you might become even more competitive.

_____

_____

_____

There you have the first two components of the business success formula: Your Passion + Felt Need. We'll uncover the third component in the next chapter.

For Reflection and Discussion

1. What are some issues both of you feel passionately about? List as many as come to mind, then number them in order of importance.

_____

_____

_____

2. What are some felt needs you observe as you look around your own home, your neighborhood, the world around you? List as many as you can.

_____

_____

_____

_____

3. Now, evaluate which of your passions most closely corresponds to a felt need in the marketplace. What possible business ideas do you conceive?

_____

_____

_____

5

Your Business Plan: Something to Point to ... Other Than Each Other

WE DEFINE *BUSINESS PLAN* as "a clearly defined target, pinned to the wall, which couples can point at, rather than pointing the finger at each other." If your business plan accomplishes nothing else, it will give you something handy to crumple into a ball and throw at your mate the next time you get frustrated! It will also force you to clarify what you are in business to do, how and when you are going to do it, and who is going to do what. And, not surprisingly, it happens to be the final component in our Business Success Formula:

BUSINESS SUCCESS FORMULA:
YOUR PASSION + FELT NEED + SOLID PLAN
= SUCCESS

While researching this book, we were amazed to discover how few couples actually had a formal business plan. And not only fledgling start-ups, but also successful, well-established businesses were operating without a written plan. "In our seventeen years in business, we never had a business plan," says Gail Hayden, who operates The Fragrance Shop and The Golden Pineapple, an herb farm and country craft shop. "We didn't plan it, we just did it."

The Shells, co-owners of Tumbleweed Upholstery, are also typical. "Our plan is to get rich and enjoy life. We have nothing written down. However, Dennis has a very detailed plan in his head. We've been too busy to write anything down." Their informal approach works. "We have exceeded our annual income goal and it's only July. It looks like we'll probably double our income goal by the end of the year."

Clearly, a business can survive without a business plan. However, that is the exception, not the rule. A well-defined plan will make the path much smoother and will definitely reduce conflict. As one woman said, "Heaven help the couple who constantly debates direction." Besides, it shouldn't take you more than ten hours of intensive work to write one, and the exercise itself is extremely valuable, whether you've been in business ten minutes or ten years.

The Basics of Your Business Plan

It doesn't have to be elaborate, but we are convinced every business needs a solid business plan—*in writing*. Paolo and Margo Pignatelli, owners of The Corner Store, rely on a one-page business plan, which Paolo says was well worth the effort of preparing. "We sat down and determined where we wanted to go. We were looking for an option that would give us income but still let us be available for our children. We also wanted a business we can eventually pass along to our children and enrich them in the process."

The Corner Store specializes in helping people capitalize on their intellectual property. "We felt strongly that people should get paid for their intellectual work— that's only right. Too often, that doesn't happen. We knew we could make a difference and felt a strong sense of mission about it." So the Pignatellis had *Duck #1* in order: they were building on Passion.

Second, they looked at the market to determine where felt needs existed. "My specialty is mathematics and computer science," says Paolo. "So I developed a clear vision of where I think computers are going in the next five years. We decided to capitalize on those trends, but knew we couldn't do it alone. So we sat down and decided what alliances we needed, and then developed a strategy for pursuing them. We then clearly defined what we had to offer in return." That took care of *Duck #2*: Felt Need.

Now to get that final duck in order, Paolo recalls, "I simply took out a yellow pad and wrote down where we were, where we wanted to be, and then filled in the middle. It took me three full days of very concentrated work, but when I typed it up, it was only a page and a half long." The brevity doesn't phase them, though. "Every word is strategic," they insist. "A business plan doesn't have to be long, it just has to be right. It has to be specific and achievable, and it must be the fruit of careful analysis." Presto! The elusive *Duck #3*: a Plan.

As an added bonus, the Pignatellis have actually been able to *memorize* their entire business plan, because it is so concise. Paolo admits, "I'm an idea person, so it's tempting for me to wake up every day with a new idea and chase after it. I could really dissipate my energies. The business plan helps me train my mind to focus energy on activities that lead to a specific goal. When I start drifting into new areas, I always come back to the plan and remind myself: 'This is the business I'm in.' "

The Pignatellis also insist that their business plan has virtually eliminated the type of conflict that is typical in most husband-wife partnerships. "We don't even have to discuss anything. We proceed with absolutely no fear. We clearly divided the work. Margo does what she's been assigned, and I do what I'm assigned. It's very clear, so there is absolutely no conflict at all. Working together is completely harmonious." Now, wouldn't you like to say that? Then write a clear business plan. (Either that or trade in your beloved spouse for a kinder, gentler model.) The next time you are tempted to point the finger at your spouse, point at the plan instead! It will be good for your business and good for your marriage. Just do it!

Transitioning Your Business From Part-time to Full-Time

If at all possible, your business plan should reflect your intention to start small and grow gradually. Ideally, you should hang on to the security of a full-time job as long as needed. Of course, the transition can be quite tricky. How do you balance it all when your business finally begins to take off? How do you know when to quit your day job? How do you know whether the boom in your business is a short-term fluke or proof positive that you've got a winner on your hands? Frankly, it's hard to tell. And since we are both conservative, we recommend that you err on the side of caution.

Following is a minimum-risk approach to planning the transition from a part-time to a full-time business:

1. Build a six- to twelve-month financial cushion.

If you aren't willing to take calculated risks, you shouldn't be an entrepreneur. It comes with the territory. On the other hand, the entrepreneurial arena is no place for foolishness, either. To play it safe—and to give yourself room to maneuver and enough financial security to actually sleep at night—we recommend setting aside six to twelve months' worth of living and business expenses.

How long it takes you to build that cushion will determine how long you absolutely must hang on to that wearisome day job. If you've got the money from day one and you want to plunge full speed ahead into the business venture, give it a try. However, you better have a mighty strong stomach and nerves of steel.

2. *Use free-lancers or temporary services to handle overflow until you're sure the work increase is permanent.*

Most entrepreneurs are given to fits of enthusiasm; by and large, we're a pretty optimistic bunch. Unfortunately, that optimism can sometimes impair our decision-making apparatus. The minute business picks up we think our prayers have been answered. It ain't necessarily so. Take it from those who have been down in the trenches. If there's one thing you can count on when you go into business for yourself, it is this: you can't count on anything!

So, when business suddenly booms, resist the temptation to quit your day job. And definitely resist the temptation to immediately hire employees. Instead, turn to temporary help services, free lancers, and independent contractors who will work for you on an as-needed basis. Corporations call this outsourcing; we just call it smart business practice.

3. *Work evenings and weekends.*

We're not sure how to break the bad news to you, but your life will probably get a whole lot worse before it gets better. Keeping your day job will mean that, at least in the beginning, you'll have to work evenings and weekends. Your personal life will cease to exist and your family life will almost certainly suffer. That's why you absolutely, positively must choose a business you love! Your life will be miserable enough during the transition from full-time employment to full-time self-employment. Don't make matters worse by choosing the wrong business.

Wouldn't it be easier to just quit your day job and leap into your new business? Yes, it certainly would.

68

And if you have the cash flow and confidence to make such a move, then by all means, do it. Otherwise, brace yourself for some tough days ahead.

4. Cut back your day job to part-time.

Not every job lends itself well to this strategy, but if it works for you, it's a great option. Once your business begins progressing well, cut back to part-time or at least eliminate any overtime you have been working. This way, you'll have the best of both worlds: a steady (albeit somewhat smaller) paycheck, plus enough time and energy to develop your business.

5. Take a part-time job, if needed.

If scaling back to part-time in your current job is not an option, you might try landing a part-time job elsewhere. This provides the same benefits as above.

6. Involve your children whenever and however possible.

Once upon a time, children played a vital role in the economic survival of the family. Once upon a time, children felt needed. Now, children are often treated like pets: we feed them, we entertain them, and sometimes they entertain us. We enjoy having them around (usually), but we don't *need* them and they know it. If the truth were known, most kids would tell you they yearn to play a vital role in the family. They need to know they are needed. What an opportunity your family business presents to fill this inner desire.

By involving your children, you can free yourself up to work on those things that only you can do. Let your preschoolers open the mail and then color all over the envelopes. Let your elementary-age children take partial responsibility for packing and shipping. Teach your high-schoolers how to run a business.

7. Don't burn any bridges.

Whatever you do during the transition from employment to self-employment, don't burn any bridges. When you quit your job, give ample notice and leave graciously. You never know who may need your products or services in the future. You never know who may know someone who knows someone, etc. Your reputation can be made or destroyed, depending upon the way you handle the leaving of any job.

Making the Transition From Sole Proprietor to Partnership

Another crucial issue to address during the business planning phase is determining the point at which you can move the business from a one-man (or one-woman) operation to a couple-run business. More to the point, what will it take for the business to generate enough revenue to provide financially for the family. Here are some specific milestones to watch for and plan for:

1. Billable hours

If you are in a service business, it doesn't matter how many hours you work. What does matter is how many hours you *bill*. Calculate the number of hours per month you need to bill to make the business profitable enough to pay both your home and business expenses. (And hopefully a few extras!) Consider the following example of a typical one-month expense estimate:

Family Budget:	$2,500
Business Operating Budget:	$2,500
Profit Margin 20%:	400
Income Needed:	$5,400

If your hourly rate is fifty dollars, you will need to bill 108 hours per month, or twenty-seven hours per week. Once you consistently bill thirty hours per week for six consecutive months, your spouse should feel very comfortable about quitting his or her job to join the firm.

2. Financial goals

If you don't bill hourly, you can develop alternative ways to gauge your financial success. Product sales are actually easier to evaluate than billable hours. Let's assume your family has the same income need as above ($5,400), and you sell a product that yields ten dollars profit per sale. You should consistently sell 540 units per month if you expect to sleep easy at night. So, you might set a financial goal of six hundred units per month for six straight months before your spouse joins the firm.

3. Number of customers

Some businesses, such as public relations, operate on a flat-fee basis. For example, a typical monthly retainer for public relations services runs between $1,000 to $2,500 per month. Depending upon your business and family budget, your goal could be to sign five customers to six-month contracts. At that point, you'll need all the help you can get and you can well afford to hire your spouse.

4. Expert status

When you become "the" person to talk to about your industry; when you receive a steady flow of invitations to speak at conferences; when expert-wanna-be's start calling you for advice; when you enter a room and strangers *know you*, you can consider yourself an emerging expert. And that's a sure sign your business is about to take off, if it hasn't already.

5. Gaining publicity

A critical measure of your status as an expert in your field is media coverage. One of the best indicators of future business success is the current level of publicity you are using and/or receiving. You should aggressively pursue media publicity: newspapers, magazines, radio, television. When your efforts start paying off with requests for articles and interviews, you are on your way.

6. *Strong percentage of repeat business*

When customers keep coming back for more, you know you've got a good thing going. It will be only a matter of time before the word gets out and people start beating a path to your door. Perhaps all that's needed for rapid business expansion at this time is the hiring of your spouse to help people find your door via an aggressive marketing campaign.

7. *Steady flow of customer referrals*

There's only one indicator that's even better than repeat business: referral business. When your customers believe in you enough to send others your way, you've discovered a magic formula for success.

Who Gets Paid What?

Once both husband and wife are officially in the business, they will need to deal with the dicey issue of who gets paid what. How will the profits, assets, and liabilities be legally divided? In community property states, all assets acquired during a marriage belong equally to both husband and wife, whether they are in business together or not. However, in most states, a couple may set up whatever division of property they prefer. A natural choice might be a fifty-fifty split, but legally, the company may be divided any way you like.

Many accountants advise couples to pay a substantial salary to one partner, and pay the other (usually the woman) little or nothing. This strategy can save money in Social Security taxes, and possibly also in unemployment benefits, disability, and health insurance plans.

What about the intangible effects of such a decision? How will the unpaid or low-paid partner feel about his or her value to the company? While it may cost extra to compensate both spouses equally or according to their contribution to the company, it may be more profitable, in the long run, to do so. Why? Because a person who feels valued will contribute more to the company than a person who does not feel valued. If a wife can work enthusiastically without pay, God bless her and save the taxes. But if it causes her to resent either the business or her husband, then pay her what she's worth. It's important, here, to distinguish between *compensation* and *ownership*. For example, the wife may receive no salary but still *own* fifty percent or more of the company. Consult your accountant before making any compensation or ownership decisions.

Business Planning Software

Thanks to the wide range of computerized programs now available, preparing a business plan is not nearly as demanding as it once was. These relatively inexpensive programs can walk you through the process and help create a professional-looking plan. Following is a collection of the best software currently available:

BizPlan Builder
JIAN Tools for Sales, Inc.
800–346–5426
List: $129

Business Plan Toolkit*
Palo Alto Software
800–229–7526
List: $150

Destiny Business Information and Planning System*
Planet Corp.
800–366–5111
List: $250

---

*Chosen a "Best Buy" by the editors of *Home Office Computing*.

PFS: Business Plan
SoftKey International
800–227–5609
List: $80

PlanMaker
PowerSolutions for Business
800–955–3337
List: $129

PlanWrite
Business Resource Software
800–423–1228
List: $130

Success, Inc.
Dynamic Pathways
800–543–7788
List: $130

For Reflection and Discussion

Following is a sample outline for your business plan. Remember, it doesn't have to be long, it just has to be right. Unless, of course, you decide to seek a loan. In that case, you'll need a much more elaborate plan. (Note: We'll deal with the issue of loans in detail in the next chapter.) For now, use the following as a guide for your plan:

Sample Business Plan Outline

1. Describe the proposed business in detail: the product or service you plan to offer and the potential customers.
2. Describe your credentials.
3. Analyze the competitiveness of your product or service (in comparison to specific competitors).
4. Identify needed supplies and equipment.
5. Identify funding sources.
6. Prepare a proposed budget.
7. Prepare a thorough marketing plan.

6
Minimize Your Risk of Failure

BUSINESS FAILURE IS not a mystery. Research has revealed very precisely how entrepreneurs get into trouble. Here's the breakdown:

Major Causes of Business Failure[1]

Inexperience and Incompetence	87.0%
Reason Unknown	7.2%
Neglect	1.8%
Disaster	1.4%
Fraud	1.2%
Other	1.4%

The bottom line is this: the American educational system does not train people to become entrepreneurs or business owners. It trains students to become employees. Think back to your own educational experience. Where you taught *any* of the skills you now need to succeed in your own business? If so, you are very rare indeed. Most of us were taught to arrive on time, sit down and shut up. We were expected to do exactly as we were told and to do nothing until we received specific

---

[1] *The Home & Family Business Workshop Workbook*, by Greg Harris, 1992, p. 3.

instructions concerning the next step. As for developing solutions, we were instructed to "parrot back" the *one* right answer as previously dictated by teacher or textbook.

The above skills are very valuable, indeed, if you want to earn a regular paycheck in a factory or an office. However, they are entirely inadequate for running your own business. Unfortunately, for many entrepreneurs, inexperience and incompetence often prevail and business failure follows.

What do we mean by inexperience and incompetence—the number one reason businesses fail? Dun & Bradstreet reports some of the most common business mistakes as follows:[2]

- Inadequate Sales
- Competitive Weakness
- Heavy Operating Expenses
- Receivables Difficulties
- Inventory Difficulties
- Excessive Fixed Assets
- Poor Location

All of these mistakes are easily avoided and can always be overcome. The secret to real success, of course, is *not to make these mistakes in the first place*. With that in mind, let's discuss some ways to minimize the risk of failure.

Join Forces With a Franchise or Direct Selling Organization

One of the major advantages of buying into a franchise or direct sales organization is that experienced people have already paved the way. They will tell you exactly how to run the business: how to sell, how to deal with competition, how to control expenses, and how to

---

[2]Ibid.

collect payments. If you need to open a storefront, the franchise will conduct the market research necessary to determine the right location.

Woody and Dayna Brohm operated a McMaid franchise and said the experience was invaluable. "They [the parent company] knew exactly what do to and how to do it. There was a system for everything, from marketing to managing the people and the paperwork. We didn't sit around guessing and hoping we were right because the people who'd gone before us had established a proven track record. On the few occasions we thought we knew better and tried doing it our way, we were proven wrong. We quickly learned to trust their advice."

The McMaid business was profitable. However, the Brohms didn't enjoy managing employees. So they started an appliance repair business; Dayna manages the appointments and paperwork and Woody does the repairs. "Even though the franchise wasn't quite right for us, we wouldn't trade that experience for anything. It was like getting an MBA in entrepreneurship. Everything we learned from the franchise we are applying to our new business. If we had tried to start our first business from scratch, it would have been a disaster."

Without question, sales training is the most important type of instruction a franchise or direct selling organization can provide. Knowing how to sell your product is absolutely critical, because thirty-nine percent of failed businesses report that inadequate sales were the major cause of their demise.[3] Have you ever had *any* sales training? If the answer is no, you might want to investigate the training sources in your area. We often encourage people to work with a direct selling organization that has a solid sales training program. Even if you decide later to launch another business, you'll dramatically increase your chances for success.

Gary Reichart, who operates three network market-

---

[3]Ibid.

ing businesses with his wife, says he was attracted to network marketing because it had very little risk. "The only thing you can lose is time and energy; financially, there just isn't much risk. Most programs you can get into for less than $500, many for less than $100. Within an hour you can be in business; within days you can be making money. That's what I call low risk and minimum effort."

Whether you choose a franchise, a direct sales company, or a network marketing organization, the company will supply you with all needed products. They have already done research and development for you; they have evaluated the competition and set product prices accordingly. In our work with entrepreneurs, we've found pricing to be one of the most challenging issues they face.

Another advantage of working with a direct sales company is that all materials (catalogs, price lists, order forms) and marketing strategies are provided for you. As a professional copywriter and former ad agency executive, Donna can testify how incredibly expensive and time-consuming it is to develop such materials. It could cost you anywhere from $10,000 to $30,000 to develop top-quality marketing materials. Even if you have that much money on hand, do you really possess the expertise to oversee such a project?

"We don't have to produce any marketing materials; the corporation has all that at our disposal. They also do advertising for us, and put together product information. It makes us look much more professional and enables us to concentrate on building up our business. They've invested time and money so we can be more efficient," says Judy Irmen. She and her husband have been Amway distributors since 1991. They are now at the Ruby Direct Distributor level, which means they've generated enough income to support both of them full-time.

The Role of Debt in Business Failure

Evidence clearly proves a direct correlation between the level of debt incurred by a business and the likelihood the business will fold. The vast majority of businesses that fail have from $5,000 and $25,000 worth of debt. Successful businesses start small, and build up gradually.

Much has been made of the success of women entrepreneurs. And, it's true, women have a better track record in starting successful enterprises than men. The innate superiority of women certainly plays a key role (just kidding). However, we think the real reason women are more successful is because they have had limited access to capital. Before the credit crunch—and sometimes even today—it was *too easy* for men to get loans. All a man needed was his navy blue suit, white shirt and red tie, and the local banker would lend him $50,000 for whatever scheme he had cooked up while driving home on the freeway. As a result, the majority of businesses started by men fail.

Women have traditionally found it difficult to get a business loan. Even the most dazzling business plan, with the niftiest spreadsheets imaginable, wasn't enough to persuade skittish bankers. As a result, women were forced to start small and to rely on their own creativity. They analyzed each move with great care. They learned to stay close to their customers, to shift with the demands of the market. If one approach or product didn't work, she quickly changed strategies. Making adjustments is much more difficult if you have already manufactured $20,000 worth of inventory on borrowed money.

In contrast, it has been our observation that a man with a loan is a man who isn't going to change much. Even when everything around him indicates his idea is not working, he'll hold on to the bitter end. As we often say in our seminars, "It's hard to listen to your instincts when the banker is screaming in the other ear." Before you go out seeking a loan, consider the following chart:

Percentage Distribution of Business Failures by Size of Debt[4]

Size of Liability	Percentage of Failures
Under $5,000	4.6%
$5,000 to $25,000	32.8%
$100,000 to $1,000,000	19.7%
Over $1,000,000	1.7%

If you are already deeply in debt as a family, we suggest you begin to seriously deal with that problem before launching your business enterprise. For information on getting your debt under control and other money management issues, we encourage you to contact Christian Financial Concepts at 404–534–1000. CFC is a Christian ministry founded by noted financial author, Larry Burkett. This organization offers everything from books and tapes to seminars and no-hidden-agenda financial counseling.

The Role of Time in Business Failures

In the following chart, you will notice that the vast majority of businesses fail during the first five years; in fact, a significant number of *those* actually fail in the first two years. The reason is self-evident: the owners lacked the experience that only time will bring. Once again, we see the importance of starting slow and starting small. Your mistakes become valuable lessons, rather than the making of a catastrophe. As Greg Harris, owner of Christian Life Workshops and several other business enterprises, notes: "By starting and managing

---

[4]Ibid. Original source: Dunn & Bradstreet.

your own businesses without borrowing money from strangers, you give yourself the needed time to gain business experience and competence."

Harris believes, "Many of these young businesses could have succeeded in time. Unfortunately, an impatient creditor shut them down prematurely." The only way to avoid that pitfall is by allowing the business to be *self-funding*.

So how do you get the money to start a business, if going into debt is not an option? Why not fund your business the old-fashioned way? Savings.

You may have $100, $1,000, or $10,000 in savings you want to invest. But only invest dollars you can afford to lose. You may consider borrowing money from a close relative, but be sure it's an amount you can repay even if the business fails.

No matter where you get the money from, we advocate starting *small*.

The Average Number of Years Before Business Failure[5]

Years	% of Failures
5 or less	53.2%
6–10	24.4%
Over 10	22.4%

The Role of Budgeting in Business Failure

When it comes to budgeting, you need to decide two things: first, how much you *will* spend and *no less*, and second, how much you *can* spend and *no more*. At the risk of promoting stereotypes, we've found that women usually err on one side of the spectrum, while men are at the other extreme.

You can probably guess at which end of the spectrum we'll usually find the men. It seems that as soon as he gets his loan, the man's out looking for office space to

---

[5]Ibid.

rent at $2,000 per month. Then, he thinks he needs a secretary and new office equipment. By the way, do you know what the most dangerous place in America is? OF-FICEMAX! You go in to pick up a bottle of Wite-out™, and the next thing you know, your basket is loaded with computer peripherals. Later, you're wondering what happened to the office-supply budget. Gentleman, be on guard.

Women, typically, are on the opposite end of the spectrum. They tend to second-guess themselves too much and can be reluctant to invest in their businesses. Rather than loading up the cart at OfficeMax, they'll stand with the bottle of Wite-out™ in hand, debating, "Should I really buy this? After all, we do need bread. I don't know; it's a tough call. Wite-out . . . bread . . . hmmm. . . ."

Of course, we are exaggerating these stereotypes . . . just a tad! The point is: you shouldn't recklessly blow your budget, but you shouldn't operate without a budget, either. It is absolutely vital that you and your spouse decide on Day One exactly how much you are willing to invest in the business. Do you believe in this business $500 worth, $5,000 worth? Maybe you have an extra $50,000 lying around. The point is, identify your sources of funds, allocate them in advance, and try to stay within your budget as much as possible.

Lack of Self-Management Skills

The American educational system does not train us to be our own boss, or to become self-managers. Instead, we are taught the secret to success is towing the academic line, getting a college degree, maybe even an MBA. Then, we simply need to find an employer to take care of us. (And if he won't take care of us, the government better!)

To make it on your own, you will have to leave behind what Paul and Sarah Edwards call "the paycheck mentality." Before you can reap the benefits of self-employment, you must learn to manage both yourselves and your business. If you suspect mismanagement could be a potential pitfall for you, we strongly recommend the Edwardses' book *Making It on Your Own* (Jeremy Tarcher, 1991). In fact, all their books are outstanding tools for learning to manage your own business. They include: *Working From Home, Getting Business to Come to You* and *The Best Home Businesses for the 90's*. All are widely available in bookstores.

Marketing Naiveté

Marketing is another subject our educational system fails to adequately teach. Each year, *Home Office Computing Magazine* conducts a survey among its half-million readers. And year after year, the topic readers want to know more about is marketing. You may have the greatest product or service in the history of human civilization, but if you don't know how to land customers, you won't have much of a business. There's no such thing as *too much* marketing savvy.

In the resource section of this book, we've listed the very best books on small business marketing. Among the very, very best are books written by Jay Conrad Levinson, who developed the concept of "Guerrilla Marketing." His basic premise is this: in order to compete with the mighty marketing armies of corporate America, the small business owner has to wage war like a guerrilla fighter. We have followed much of his advice and found his techniques to be extremely effective.

Employee Problems

There's just no way around it. When you hire employees, you hire problems. Responses from the couples featured in this book ranged from "we'd rather die than hire an employee," to eloquent statements regarding the value of third-party input, and the joys of providing employment for people in the community.

Whether you consider employees a joy or a sorrow, they do create a whole new set of challenges. Employee theft, employee lawsuits, and employee incompetence are all extremely important issues to consider before adding non-family members to the payroll. They may live by a different set of values or pursue goals that conflict with the values and goals of the company you are building. Come to think of it, you better explore these issues before hiring family members, too!

Staying Alert to Pitfalls

We will have much more to say about business success in the following chapters. For now, stay alert to the pitfalls discussed here. Stay out of debt. Allow enough time (by starting small) to learn how to be a small business owner. Research your business thoroughly. Hire employees only after much deliberation. Examine your motives and steer clear of any business deal that smacks of a get-rich-quick mentality. Become a student of marketing and learn all you can about marketing yourself and your business. Do these things, and you are well on your way to success.

For Reflection and Discussion

1. Are you willing to stay out of debt—at least as far as possible, and especially during the first five years?
2. Are you willing to give yourself the time you need to succeed? Even if it means keeping your day job a bit longer? Even if it means starting slow?
3. Will you proceed with caution before hiring employees?
4. What steps will you take to become a self-taught expert on marketing? Consider books, cassette tapes, seminars, consultations.

PART THREE

GETTING ALONG WITH EACH OTHER

7
Which Type of Partner Are You?

JIM AND NAOMI RHODE are two totally different people who are absolutely intent on maximizing each other's natural gifts. "Early in our marriage, we recognized that our opposite characteristics provided everything we needed for a successful business package. We worked together as a team raising children and pursuing hobbies, and that worked well for us. So why wouldn't it work well in a business? It just made sense." Indeed, it did make sense . . . and a lot of cents, too.

Twenty-three years ago, the Rhodes created a professional speaking and consulting business, SmartPractice. Today, their multi-multi-million dollar business employs 280 people. (They didn't want us to disclose the exact dollar figure; trust us, it's extremely impressive!)

Naomi Rhode is very organized. She prepares her speeches well in advance. She plans, she scripts, she organizes. She spends hours practicing and honing her delivery. Not Jim Rhode. He likes to fly by the seat of his pants. He picks up the *Wall Street Journal* on the day of his talk and tells the audience what it means for their business tomorrow.

"I *inspire* them to change, then Jim tells them *how* to

change in a very down-to-earth, common sense way," explains Naomi. "I come back and inspire them again; he comes back with more 'how to' information. It's literally a one-two punch. The audience is accessing both the left [analytical] and the right [creative] sides of their brain. That maximizes their learning and our effectiveness. Jim and I both know we wouldn't be as effective without the other."

In the beginning, Naomi had a rough time dealing with Jim's work style. "It took me a few years, but I have come to accept our differences. If I worry about him, I pay the price. He is not going to change, so nagging is useless. We have an understanding: I'll be responsible for what I said I'd be responsible for. And he'll be responsible for what he is responsible for. We just have to trust each other to come through. If you *can't* trust each other to come through, you've got a whole different set of problems. If you have a lack of trust, you have a fundamental problem."

The Rhodes have come to place full confidence in each other's ability to come through . . . both for the audience and for each other. "The real key, I think, is a genuine belief that the other person has more to contribute than you do," says Naomi. "He genuinely believes the audience needs me; I *know* the audience needs him. We believe that completely."

Opposites Attract

Everyone knows opposites attract. Most likely, you and your spouse are two very different people. No doubt that's been a source of friction in your marriage. Now it's time to be thankful for those differences. As the French say, *Viva la différence.* It takes a broad range of gifts to run a successful business. If your spouse were just like you, your business venture would be doomed to failure. Nevertheless, the very differences that create balance and equip you for success can also create conflict.

Understanding why your spouse acts the way he or she does can help promote harmony in your marriage and in your business relationship. To that end, numerous philosophers, psychologists, and theologians have developed theories of personality to explain why we do what we do. The oldest system was developed by the ancient Greeks who divided people into four temperaments: Choleric, Sanguine, Phlegmatic, and Melancholy.

More recently, Lee Ellis, Director of Career Pathways, developed a system based on the DISC (Dominant, Influencing, Steady, and Conscientious) personality assessment system. The following charts are adapted from his book *Your Career in Changing Times* (Moody Press, 1993), co-authored with Larry Burkett.

Rate yourself on a scale of one to ten, with ten being the highest. On the vertical scale, ten means you are very extroverted, and zero means you are very introverted. On the horizontal scale, ten means you are very formal, while zero means you are very informal. When you are finished rating yourself, connect the dots. The interpretation of your charts are on the following pages. No peeking!

You have just plotted your personality type. Now read on to find out the strengths and weaknesses associated with your type. Lee Ellis of Career Pathways provides the following overview of the four behavioral tendencies.

HUSBAND'S PERSONALITY CHART

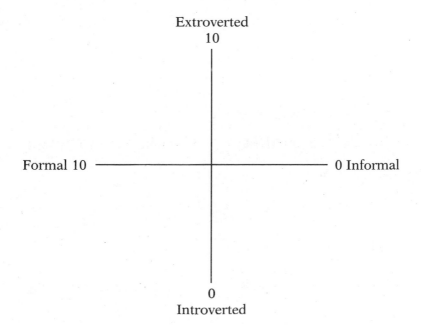

WIFE'S PERSONALITY CHART

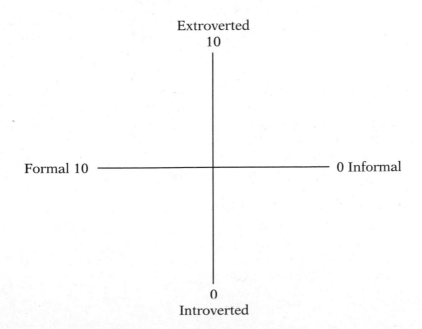

PERSONALITY KEY

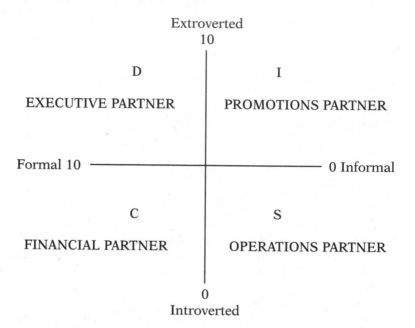

Extroverted
10

D

EXECUTIVE PARTNER

I

PROMOTIONS PARTNER

Formal 10 ──────────────── 0 Informal

C

FINANCIAL PARTNER

S

OPERATIONS PARTNER

0
Introverted

DISC Profile: Four Behavioral Tendencies

- **D=DOMINANT.** "People who have a high level of dominance are naturally motivated to control their environments," says Ellis. "They are usually assertive, independent, confident, pioneering, direct, and strong-willed. They are typically bold and not afraid to take strong action to get the desired results. They are very driven to reach specific goals. They function best in a challenging environment." We call this type of person the "Executive Partner."

- **I=INFLUENCING.** "People who are highly influencing are naturally driven to relate to others," according to Ellis. "Usually they are talkative, cheerful, friendly, persuasive, fun-loving, and optimistic. They are typically enthusiastic motivators and will seek out others to help them accomplish results. They are also high-spirited and usually quite popular. Tending to be more emotional, they function best in a favorable environment." This is the "Promotions Partner" or "Promoter."

- S=STEADY. "People who have a high level of steadiness are naturally motivated to cooperate with and support others," explains Ellis. "They are usually patient, consistent, considerate, loyal, and very dependable. Being pleasant and easygoing makes them excellent team players. They are especially productive when working in a supportive environment." This is the "Operations Partner."

- C=CONSCIENTIOUS. "People with a high level of conscientiousness (or cautiousness) are focused on doing things right," says Ellis. "Usually they are detail-oriented, reserved, self-disciplined, and find it easy to follow prescribed guidelines. Typically they strive for accuracy and quality and, therefore, set high standards for themselves and others." They function best in a structured environment. You've just met the "Financial Partner."

Strengths and Weaknesses

Each of the personality types has both strengths and weaknesses. None is better than another. None is more important to the success of your business than another. What *is* critical to the success of your business is a clear understanding of who's who and why they act the way they do. Once you understand your spouse's personality type, try to adapt your style to bring out the best in each other. The following guidelines will get you started:

EXECUTIVE PARTNER
Strengths
If you want to get a job done, ask the Executive Part-

ner to take control of the situation. And will he ever. He'll quickly set goals and make decisions, rather than wait around to see what anyone else wants to do. He'll do more than keep busy, he'll actually get things done. You never have to wonder what the Executive Partner is really thinking or feeling; he'll let you know right up front. He is a great problem solver and can fix whatever is broken with the utmost of confidence—even if he has never faced that particular set of circumstances before.

As a natural-born entrepreneur, you can count on the Executive Partner to bounce back when something goes wrong in the business. If one strategy bombs or one deal falls through, he'll quickly set to work on the next project and pursue it with equal vigor. And you can count on him to continually introduce new ideas and enthusiastically initiate new projects. His energy seems almost unlimited and his ability to get things done is remarkable.

He likes to win, to be the best, and he'll work hard to make sure the business is the best it can be. And because the Executive Partner is a visionary, he'll be able to determine what's best, not only in the short term, but down the road as well.

Weaknesses

Problems begin when the Executive Partner tries to take too much control of the business. He can be quite the dictator. He has a tendency to act first and think things through afterward. This can really cause trouble if he initiates projects without making a realistic assessment of how much time and effort will be required to complete them. The Executive Partner is great at getting things started; he's not so great at finishing them. He tends to jump from project-to-project and leave the detailed cleanup and follow-through work to his partner. And because he is overly demanding, he expects his partner to finish up quickly.

He can be overbearing and inconsiderate of the feelings of others. For example, he'll move ahead with new projects without seeking his partner's advice or approval. He loves to talk and tends to forget that other people have important things to say, too.

PROMOTIONS PARTNER

Strengths

Who can resist the Promoter? Her bright cheery smile and her bubbly personality make her the life of the party or networking event. She loves to laugh and has a good time doing just about anything. In fact, she has so much fun promoting her business, it doesn't feel like work. Don't be deceived by mere appearances. Her networking savvy is absolutely critical to business success.

The Promoter can talk to anyone, anywhere, at any time, about almost anything. The eternal optimist, she always expects the best from people and from life. She's a trusting soul who sees only the best in others and is quick to overlook their weaknesses. If you hire employees, they will love working for the Promoter.

Thanks to her incredible verbal skills, she is great at persuading others to her point of view. That can't help but boost the business's bottom line. When she feels passionately about something—whether it's a product or a cause—she easily wins people to her side and inspires them to get involved. She is the consummate networker and actively cultivates contacts who can lend support to the business.

In our experience, it is extremely common for women Promoters to start a business which will grow rapidly, but then require management savvy they do not possess. Once these women recruit their husbands, who are usually Financial or Operations oriented, their businesses become wildly successful. Although we did not conduct a scientific study, we did do extensive research and conducted nearly one hundred interviews. Almost every successful husband-and-wife team had an outstanding Promoter—often the wife—and a silent partner to keep the Promoter on target. In our case, Donna is the Promoter/Executive, while Cameron is the Operations/Financial Partner.

Weaknesses

Although the Promoter will do a great job of attracting new customers, she may not be the ideal person to run the business. Why? Because she tends to be disorganized and rarely takes time for in-depth planning. She is easily distracted and has a difficult time finishing what she starts.

The most common criticism of the Promoter, of course, is that she talks too much. She just can't stop talking! When you work for someone else, you are given a paycheck even if you waste part of the day chatting on the phone. (There may be a limit to your boss's patience, however.) When you are in business for yourself, you have no such luxury. The Promoter must learn to channel her talkativeness in a productive direction or her business is doomed. The real danger, especially for Promoters who work at home, lies in personal phone calls and friends who drop by during the day. These can steal precious time away from the business.

It is possible for the Promoter to actually be so optimistic that she becomes just plain unrealistic. She tends to be a poor judge of character because she takes people at face value without looking at their underlying motivations. Unfortunately, there is an unending parade of unsavory characters who prey upon new business owners. The Promoter can easily waste countless hours, expend untold energy, and lose unspeakable amounts of money chasing after the wind. (This is the voice of experience speaking!)

Also, the Promoter has a need to be accepted and therefore finds it almost impossible to say no. If Donna had a dollar for every bit of free advice and information she has given away since starting the business in 1988, we would be millionaires! (OK, so we exaggerate.) Unfortunately, people who want something for nothing are rarely grateful and their *requests* for help quickly turn into unending *demands* for help. This will drain needed time and energy away from more profitable activities.

One final warning about the Promoter: don't put her in charge of the company treasury. Money flows through her hands like water. The Promoter can become a very successful business owner, provided she finds a partner who is more detail-oriented than she.

OPERATIONS PARTNER

Strengths

The Operations Partner has the corner on patience. He has his feet firmly rooted in reality and has a good sense of what it will take to get the job done. He also has the tenacity to stay with a project through to completion. The Operations Partner is one hundred percent dependable—if he says he will take care of something, it is as good as done.

The Operations Partner thrives on routine and will no doubt have a rigid daily schedule, even if he works out of the home. He goes about tasks in a consistent manner and isn't tempted to follow after every new trend that comes along.

In terms of his interpersonal relationships, he thrives on harmony and will do whatever he can to maintain it. He will adapt his working style to suit whomever he is with and is therefore the ultimate team player. (You will notice in the following chapter on "Coping With Conflict" that the Operations Partner can get along well with any of the other personality types.)

The greatest asset of the Operations Partner is that he *actually gets things done*. He provides a sure, steady hand of quiet leadership. However, he probably prefers to play second-in-command and let someone else be the up-front person. We found that many of the men we interviewed were Operations Partners, who were extremely effective in managing the details while their

Promoter-wife won and kept the customers.

Weaknesses

Whatever else can be said about the Operations Partner, he is not naturally inclined toward entrepreneurship. In fact, he may not function well in a new enterprise, preferring instead to join the firm once it is well under way. He is not at all interested in launching new programs or product lines. He prefers to stay with the tried-and-true. In fact, he will even stay with the tried-and-found-lacking. He is slow to accept any change in procedures and fails to recognize when it's time to abandon old methods. In short, if you are looking for innovation, look elsewhere.

Another weakness of the Operations Partner is that he gets so caught up in the day-to-day details of the business he misses the big picture. Some Operations Partners can be lazy, especially in pursuing goals. Over the long term, his tendency toward bitterness may become a serious problem that spills over into the marriage. He is always there when anyone needs him, but he begins to resent the fact that people (especially his spouse/partner) are not as quick to meet his needs. He has a strong need to be appreciated. If his spouse does not voice appreciation for his quiet efforts, he feels taken advantage of and plays the victim. This dynamic is unhealthy for the business and can be deadly poisonous to the marriage.

FINANCIAL PARTNER

Strengths

The Financial Partner thrives on accuracy and aims for quality in everything she does. You can guess what her office looks like: sheer perfection. She is very detail-oriented and notices things that other people tend to overlook. She enjoys structure, discipline, and playing by the rules. No doubt she follows a set schedule each day in the office.

If there is a job to be done, she will go to any length to insure it is done properly. She has a very analytical mind and enjoys examining issues in detail. She arrives at decisions with great care and deliberation; she never does anything rash. She is the voice of reason in the often crazy world of entrepreneurship.

If you have a Financial Partner, you won't need to worry about an IRS audit: your books will be in perfect order. She is also the best person for the job when preparing your business plan and allocating scarce funds. She is very effective in analyzing the probable success of new products or services, and in determining when and how to penetrate new markets. She will make sure your business not only generates income, but actually turns a profit.

Weaknesses

The Financial Partner can often be too perfectionistic, which will cause her to have unrealistic expectations of herself and others. And because she expects perfection, she is often disappointed and becomes pessimistic. She tends to be very critical of herself and others. She is highly sensitive, picking up the slightest little insult. She has trouble forgiving and forgetting— two things essential for a couple who want to work together.

The Financial Partner is often so cautious and detail-oriented that it takes her forever to get things done. It's called "the paralysis of analysis" and can be deadly in the entrepreneurial arena where the battle goes to the swift. Unless she learns that there's not enough time to do everything perfectly and that some things only need a cursory effort, she can bring the business to a grinding halt. As the old saying goes, "Even if you are on the right track, you will get run over if you don't move."

Suggested Reading on Personality Styles

If you would like to learn more about personality theory, here are some excellent resources worth checking out:

Your Career in Changing Times. Lee Ellis and Larry Burkett, Moody Press, 1993.

Personality Plus. Florence Littauer, Fleming Revell, 1983.

Personality Puzzle. Florence and Marita Littauer, Fleming Revell, 1992.

Spirit-Controlled Temperament. Tim LaHaye, Tyndale House, 1966.

The Two Sides of Love. Gary Smalley and John Trent, Focus on the Family, 1990.

Understanding How Others Misunderstand You. Ken Voges and Ron Braund, Moody Press, 1991.

The Winning Hand: Making the Most of Your Family's Personality Differences. Wayne Rickerson, NavPress, 1991.

For Reflection and Discussion

Husband's Response to Personality Test

1. Which type best describes you?_____
2. List your five most significant strengths and describe how they will contribute to the success of your business.

Strength   Contribution

_____   _____

_____   _____

_____   _____

_____   _____

_____   _____

3. List your five most troublesome weaknesses and describe how they will interfere with your business success.

Weakness   Associated problems

_____   _____

_____   _____

_____   _____

_____   _____

_____   _____

4. List your wife's five key strengths.

Strength   Contribution

_____   _____

_____   _____

_____   _____

_____   _____

_____   _____

5. List your wife's five critical weaknesses.

Weakness   Associated problems

_____   _____

_____   _____

_____   _____

_____   _____

_____   _____

Wife's Response to Personality Test

1. Which type best describes you?_____
2. List your five most significant strengths and describe how they will contribute to the success of your business.

Strength   Contribution

_____   _____

_____   _____

_____   _____

_____   _____

_____   _____

3. List your five most troublesome weaknesses, and how they will interfere with business success.

Weakness   Associated problems

_____   _____

_____   _____

_____   _____

_____   _____

_____   _____

4. List your husband's five key strengths.

Strength   Contribution

_____   _____

_____   _____

_____   _____

_____   _____

_____   _____

5. List your husband's five critical weaknesses.

Weakness   Associated problems

_____   _____

_____   _____

_____   _____

_____   _____

_____   _____

8
Coping With Conflict

AGAIN, KEEPING IN MIND that opposites attract and given the nature of us frail human beings, it's not surprising that conflict is inevitable. This chapter explores the most likely types of conflicts you will have with your partner based on your respective DISC profiles. Remember this is not an exact science, but we found these analyses to be quite accurate. (We are again indebted to Ellis and Burkett for these insights.)

Executive Partner Conflicts With:

Executive Partner. When both husband and wife possess "executive partner" temperaments, you can count on major turf wars. They will clash over control—which both of them want and neither wants to concede. The key for this couple's survival is to clearly define territorial lines of authority. A healthy dose of mutual respect will go a long way, as well.

Promotions Partner. From the Executive's point of view, the Promoter spends too much time talking and not nearly enough time getting the job done. He wants to see results, not relationships. To ease conflict, the Promoter should emphasize the results she has achieved through forming key relationships. The Executive needs to understand and respect the importance of networking and building business alliances.

Operations Partner. The number one complaint the Executive will have about the Operations Partner is that she is not aggressive enough. Actually, he should be glad that everyone in the world is not as aggressive as he! At the same time, the "steady" spouse would probably benefit by learning a few of his partner's take-charge habits.

Financial Partner. "Don't bore me with the facts," is the Executive's battle cry, so it's not hard to understand why conflicts will occur here. The Financial Partner is extremely detail-oriented and cautious and will no doubt try to "slow down" her fast-action partner. Again, respect is the cure. There's a time for analysis and a time for action. If this couple wants to survive in business, they need to find a balanced pace that both of them can live with.

Promotions Partner Conflicts With:

Executive Partner. The Promoter becomes offended when the Executive Partner doesn't ask her opinion on important decisions. Regularly scheduled staff meetings can go a long way toward improving communication. The Executive should remember that his tendency to act now and think later has gotten him into trouble in the past. Therefore, taking time to consult his partner is not an inconvenience, but a measure of wisdom.

Promotions Partner. When two people who love the limelight get together, intense rivalry can result. Since both want to be the center of attention, bitter jealousy can develop if one starts to outshine the other. One possible solution is to divide the glow: for example, one partner can do all the radio and television interviews, while the other partner does all the schmoozing. Make it your goal to be so successful that there is enough attention and applause for everyone.

Operations Partner. These two personality types usually get along quite well. However, the Promoter tends to perceive the Operations Partner as being too sensitive and slow.

Financial Partner. Since the Promoter is the eternal optimist, she becomes very frustrated with her partner's pessimistic attitude. However, what she perceives as pessimism may be just the reality check she needs. She doesn't want to hear that her schmoozing activities are outrageously expensive, but if she doesn't listen now, there may be no business left to schmooze for. The Promoter also should remember that she tends to be a poor judge of people and situations, and therefore needs to heed the warnings of her more practical and insightful partner.

Operations Partner Conflicts With:

Executive Partner. Although the ever-polite Operations Partner won't say anything, resentment steadily builds up. He views the Executive as a self-centered, insensitive person who "steamrolls" his agenda over everyone else. The Operations Partner needs to respect the Executive's ability to get things done, while the Executive has much to learn from his more considerate counterpart.

Promotions Partner. The Promoter's tendency to talk, talk, talk can annoy the more reserved Operations Partner. The Promoter should give her partner the opportunity to work quietly. Although she may enjoy nonstop activities, she shouldn't expect the Operations Partner to keep pace with her.

Operations Partner. These two partners will get along with each other just beautifully . . . so what's the problem? They may have a very difficult time actually getting things done since neither is inclined to be a go-getter. Also, they will have difficulty making decisions because neither one wants to impose his opinion on the other. Since neither will have much flair for marketing and promotions, they may need to hire an outside person to handle that function or they won't be in business for long.

Financial Partner. This can be a very good match, especially if one or both partners have highly-sought-after technical skills. (Again, they will probably have trouble marketing themselves.) One potential problem is that the Operations Partner may view the Financial Partner as too critical and judgmental.

Financial Partner Conflicts With:

Executive Partner. The Financial Partner sometimes views the Executive as having a know-it-all attitude, which she resents. She becomes concerned when the Executive initiates plans without considering the necessary details or following established procedures. The Financial Partner needs to respect the fact that the Executive actually does know quite a bit. Because he is an entrepreneur by nature, his instincts are often right—even though he can't articulate his reasons or justify his actions. At the same time, the Executive must admit his tendency to act now and think later creates problems, not only for himself, but for those around him.

Promotions Partner. Unfortunately, there are a great many things about the Promoter that genuinely bother the Financial Partner. For example, the Promoter is disorganized and inaccurate—two of the worst crimes imaginable to the "numbers cruncher." Also, the Financial Partner thinks the Promoter is merely a "show-off" and grows impatient with her tendency to exaggerate. The best strategy for these two diametrically opposed types is a commitment to respect each other's strengths. They also need to resist the temptation to "fix" each other.

Operations Partner. The Financial Partner considers himself more productive and more disciplined than the Operations Partner. As a result, petty jealousy and a competitive spirit can creep into the business and personal relationship. Rather than comparing themselves to each other, they should measure their success by how well they compete against those outside the company. Since neither is inclined to marketing, they will need to find a way to promote their business or hire someone to do it.

Financial Partner. Mr. and Mrs. Right can equal Business-Gone-Wrong. Two Financial Partners can spend so much time arguing over who is right that they never get the job done. Like the merging of two Executives, two Financial Partners can experience very intense turf wars over control of the company. Divide and conquer is their best recourse—let each partner have control over different accounts or different aspects of the business. And, again, they had better find a way to market the business or they won't have any turf worth fighting over.

Divide the Work to Minimize Conflict

By now, you understand the unique strengths and weaknesses each spouse brings to the business partnership. Carefully work through the list at the end of this chapter and assign the responsibilities accordingly. Resist the temptation to mutter, "we can both handle it" or "we'll work it out as we go along." It is absolutely vital to your survival as business partners and spouses to determine who is responsible for what. Of course, that's only half the battle. The other half is to respect your partner's turf once it has been established and to refrain from interfering or second-guessing decisions.

Does that mean you can't provide input when asked for your opinion? No. Does it mean that you work in two separate spheres and never the twain shall meet? No. It simply means that you respect each other's expertise and authority. There's that word *respect*, again. We just can't emphasize its importance enough. Here's how Webster defines it: "to consider worthy of high regard;

esteem; *to refrain from interfering with*" (emphasis added).

When a husband and wife consider each other worthy of high regard, it is much easier to refrain from interfering with each other's work. If you do not hold your spouse in such high regard, the solution is *not* to monitor his or her efforts. Rather, the solution is not to work together at all. Respect is the foundation of your business. If that isn't rock solid, everything you try to build will eventually come crashing down around you. So, lay the foundation of respect. Then, divide and conquer!

For Reflection and Discussion

1. What do you think is most likely to cause conflict between you?

_____

_____

_____

2. List five specific strategies for preventing conflict.

_____

_____

_____

_____

_____

3. Divide responsibilities, using the following chart as a guide. There is room at the end for you to add tasks that are specific to your business.

DIVIDE AND CONQUER

His	Hers	Task
☐	☐	Marketing
☐	☐	Sales
☐	☐	Production
☐	☐	Operations (General Manager)
☐	☐	Customer correspondence
☐	☐	Computer systems: purchase and maintenance

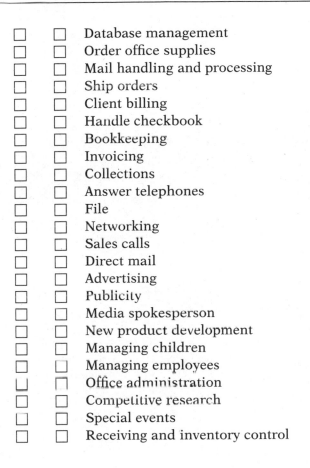

☐ ☐ Database management
☐ ☐ Order office supplies
☐ ☐ Mail handling and processing
☐ ☐ Ship orders
☐ ☐ Client billing
☐ ☐ Handle checkbook
☐ ☐ Bookkeeping
☐ ☐ Invoicing
☐ ☐ Collections
☐ ☐ Answer telephones
☐ ☐ File
☐ ☐ Networking
☐ ☐ Sales calls
☐ ☐ Direct mail
☐ ☐ Advertising
☐ ☐ Publicity
☐ ☐ Media spokesperson
☐ ☐ New product development
☐ ☐ Managing children
☐ ☐ Managing employees
☐ ☐ Office administration
☐ ☐ Competitive research
☐ ☐ Special events
☐ ☐ Receiving and inventory control

9

Communication
Skill-Builders

DR. JERRY AND MARIETTE HOLLAND know about communication; together, they have over fifty years' experience training people in the fine art of "saying what you mean and meaning what you say." Jerry has traveled around the world teaching other trainers how to train more effectively. He explains, "Clear communication is the foundation of all positive relationships, whether it's teacher-student, manager-employee, or husband-wife."

Prior to launching the Holland Center for Professional Development, the couple worked for Practical Management Associates as professional management trainers. Mariette, 57, devotes her energy to Mariette Internationale, a multi-level, direct sales organization offering cosmetics and skin care to mature women. Jerry, now in his late sixties, provides sales and communication training for Mariette's growing team of independent distributors.

"We function from the basic principle that both husband and wife are entitled to dignity and respect. It sounds so basic, but we've witnessed many couples violating this principle," says Jerry. "We are vessels of clay. We can break each other very easily—especially with the words we say." That's why the Hollands never put each other down, even in joking.

That's not to say you won't disagree with your spouse. Remember the adage, "When two people in a business always agree, one of them is unnecessary." Of course, if they disagree *all* the time, then both of them are useless. Avoid disagreeing for the sake of voicing an opinion. Remember, your relationship with your spouse is like an emotional bank account. (This concept was developed by Stephen Covey, author of *The Seven Habits of Highly Effective People.*) This is how the emotional bank account works: "Every day, we are either making deposits or withdrawals in our relationships," explains Mariette. "When we help the other person feel good about himself and about the relationship, we are making deposits to strengthen that relationship. We can never make enough deposits, because one withdrawal can wipe out all the positive emotions we've worked so hard to build. We have seen couples who constantly take and take and take until they are way overdrawn. We recognize that could happen to us."

Jerry and Mariette communicate *politely*. "If Mariette is meeting with someone in her office, that's not the time for me to bother her about what I need or want," says Jerry. "If it can wait, I let it wait. There are times when it is very inappropriate to make demands on the other person. He or she may already be under tremendous stress or may be preparing for something very important. It's simply a matter of respect; it's a way of saying: 'what you are doing is more important than what I want you to do.' When you get right down to it, the message behind interrupting is: 'you are not important. So stop what you're doing and pay attention to me and my needs.' "

We have worked closely with the Hollands over the past few years, so we know they practice what they preach. Their office is our haven of rest. They have created a wonderfully supportive work environment, and positive communication is at the heart of it. We have asked them to share their insights into what makes good communication and what types of communication styles spell trouble for a husband and wife.

The Spokesperson and the Questioner

There are two types of people in the world (can you tell we're about to make a huge generalization?): Spokespersons and Questioners. Spokespersons have a lot to say about everything—you know which Partners we mean, right? The Promoter and the Executive Partner. They say what's on their mind and like to talk, talk, talk. And that can be very annoying indeed. However, those Questioners (The Financial and Operations Partners) can be just as annoying. And they can shut down communication just as quickly. Does that strike you as contradictory? Wouldn't it seem that asking questions would *promote* conversation and good communication? Sometimes . . . but not always.

A question, for the most part, is neutral. The key is the motive behind the question. When a husband and wife work together, the Financial or Operations Partners do not ask questions just because they want to hear the Promoter or Executive Partner's opinion. They are not always interested in hearing the Spokesperson wax eloquent on a favorite subject. They ask questions with an agenda. They ask questions to gather evidence—especially evidence of the incriminating variety.

Advice to the Questioner

If you are inclined to ask your mate a lot of questions, try to examine your motives each time. Are you really interested in listening to his or her answer? Or are you conducting your own version of the Spanish Inquisition? Here are some questions to ask *yourself* before you ask your mate anything: will asking this question demonstrate a lack of trust or respect for my mate? Am I asking this question to *build up* my partner or am I looking for an opportunity to tear him or her down?

Advice to the Spokesperson

Now a word to you Spokespersons. Try to understand that your partner is not asking questions just to torment you. (Well, not always!) The Questioner is, by nature, much more cautious than you. Just think how frightening it is for the detail-oriented Financial Partner to live with a free-spirited, fly-by-the-seat-of-your-pants person like the Promoter! Yikes!!! It's not that your partner doesn't love and trust you, it's just that your risk-taking style scares him half to death. Questioners ask questions because they feel very insecure when they don't have all the facts. In most cases, they simply need reassurance that you're not going to drive the family to ruin. At least, not deliberately.

The next time your partner starts asking a litany of questions and you feel that wall of defensiveness start to rise, ask yourself: why does this question bother me? Am I trying to hide something? Is it possible that I'm not quite as sure as I'm pretending to be? Maybe the questions make you nervous because you don't have the answers. Keep alert to your natural weakness to act first and think later. Be grateful that your partner is forcing you to do something you otherwise wouldn't do: namely, think things through in a detailed, careful fashion. Your Questioning partner is a gift to you and will save you untold grief and financial loss if you will carefully ponder—then thoughtfully answer—those questions.

Just for Fun

Shortly after we wrote the initial draft of this chapter, we received a newsletter containing the following poem. It was written by a colleague of Reg and Eleonore Forder. (You met them back in Chapter 4.) See if you can figure out which one is the Questioner and which one is the Spokesperson!

Untitled Poem
by Donna C. Goodrich[1]

Eleonore, where's that mailing list?
　　Who was that on the phone?
Reg, I'm trying to get this done.
　　Can you just leave me alone!
Eleonore, how many for Advanced?
　　Where's the Beginners file?
Reg, I'm busy with this job,
　　I'll get it after a while.
Eleonore, when's Susan flying in?
　　What time do we meet Jack?
Reg, I'm typing the brochure,
　　Will you please get off my back?
Eleonore, who's coming on the cruise?
　　I haven't any notion.
Reg, if you don't give me peace,
　　I'll throw you in the ocean!
Well, we know the above's not really true
　　Of Reg and Eleonore.
And we thank God for their leadership
　　In 1994!

Fair Questions

We've never met you, so we can't predict with certainty how troublesome this conflict between the Questioner and the Spokesperson will be. We only know that it has been, without question (if you'll pardon the pun), the greatest hindrance to our working together. Cameron asks questions, questions, questions, until Donna wants to scream, scream, *scream*. And sometimes she

---

[1]Reprinted with permission from *The Christian Communicator*, January 1995.

116

does, does, does! Operating from the premise that opposites attract, we're guessing that the vast majority of couples reading this book will struggle with the Questioner-Spokesperson conflict.

Questioners like to ask questions and nothing is going to change that. Spokespersons will get annoyed—sometimes downright angry—every time they feel the question reflects a lack of trust or respect. Over the past several months, we have developed our own list of Fair and Unfair Questions. Cameron can ask any Fair Question he wants and Donna is obligated to give a thoughtful answer. However, if Cameron asks an Unfair Question, Donna can call it what it is and go on about her business.

Has this worked perfectly? No, of course not. But it has definitely reduced conflict and we encourage you to photocopy the list of Fair and Unfair Questions and keep it available as a reference.

Unfair Questions

At its core, an Unfair Question is one motivated by a desire to prove the other person wrong, stupid, inferior, untrustworthy. An Unfair Question impugns your partner's motives and puts him on the defensive.

Why did you?
Why didn't you?
Don't you know?
What were you thinking?
How can you say that?
Don't you know any better?
How could you be so stupid?
Remember the time you . . . ?
What took you so long?

Discounting Comments

It's possible to question your partner without asking a question per se. Be on guard against the following comments:

That's stupid
Don't be ridiculous
You're exaggerating
That can't be
There's no way
I doubt that very much
You never
You always
It never
It always
Every time

Fair Questions

Fair Questions demonstrate a genuine concern for your partner's well-being. They are designed to promote conversation and to get your partner to "open up" and share whatever is on his or her heart and mind. Here is a sampling:

How do you feel?
How did you feel?
Do you want to talk about it?
Is there anything I can help you with?
Is everything okay?
How can we make this better?
How should we handle it differently next time?

Powerful Statements

I apologize.
I feel badly about . . .

I hope you will forgive me for . . .
We're all human.
It's okay, honey.
Everyone makes mistakes.

Ambivalent Questions

An ambivalent question is one that can be inter-preted as either Fair or Unfair depending upon your tone of voice and body language. If these questions are fired in rapid succession, you can bet your mate will feel like an interrogation is under way. Before asking any of these questions (or similar ones) check your motives. Are you looking to build up or to tear down your part-ner?

What did he or she say?
What did you say?
What happened?
Then what happened?

Communication Strategies

Beginning with a foundation of respect and a sincere desire to build up (rather than tear down) your mate, there are additional strategies every husband-wife team can use to improve their communication skills:

Strive for Win-Win Solutions.

According to Joan Cook, a certified marriage and family therapist who works for the counseling division of Today's Family Life, "Most conflicts arise when we set our hearts upon proving 'I'm right, you're wrong. I win, you lose.' So often, couples don't listen very well. They engage in correcting and interrupting, rather than in understanding." If husband and wife will make a firm commitment to resolve all differences in a way *both* can win, the very heart of conflict will be eliminated. Instead of engaging in verbal battles, you can engage the real enemy: the problem at hand.

Keep Talking Until You Reach Agreement.

Henry Wadsworth Longfellow wrote, "A great part of the happiness of life consists not in fighting battles, but in avoiding them."[2] You can eliminate a whole lot of "verbal garbage" if both of you are absolutely committed to keep communicating until you reach agreement. With an eye on the ever-ticking clock, your mind will hone in on compromise opportunities. It's much easier to be agreeable when your goal is agreement. A great phrase to use repeatedly is, "Are we in agreement then?" The key is to break the problem down into bite-sized chunks and to come to agreement by degrees. We think a pen and paper can serve well during such lively debates.

First, write down all the things you agree on. If the mood is especially contentious, don't be afraid to start with the obvious or the humorous. Your list might look something like this:

1. We agree that we love each other.
2. We agree that we want this business to succeed.
3. We agree that divorce is not an option.
4. We agree that hiring a hit man would be very messy.
5. Therefore, we agree that resolving this conflict is in both of our best interests. We further agree not to sleep tonight until we reach agreement.

Get specific about your problem; remember to start with small items that are easy to agree on, then work your way toward the more difficult issues and decisions.

---

[2]Quotes on Line: "Words from the Wise," by Keith D. Mohler. AskSam Software, 1992.

Take Notes.

As you work through your "agreement list" you may find it helpful to listen quietly and take notes while your partner states his or her case. Then, rather than arguing your case, advocate the other person's position. Pretend you are an attorney arguing the most important case of your life. Be persuasive. Be passionate. This is an eye-opening exercise.

Put On an Act.

Jerry Holland shares an interesting conversation he once had with a professional actor. "He told me it was virtually impossible not to experience the sensation of 'falling in love' when the script called for falling in love with his co-star. That's why Hollywood romances are legendary among the hero and his leading lady. The lesson for those of us who want to stay in love is clear. When you *act* loving, you feel loving. When you say loving, kind, thoughtful things to your wife, you feel and behave more loving, kind, and thoughtful. When you communicate your love through your actions, your commitment to that person actually increases."

Go Knee-to-Knee, Not Head-to-Head.

Here's another great idea from the Hollands. "The next time you have a disagreement, sit knee-to-knee, hold hands, look into each other's eyes and then fight. It's much harder to say cruel, hateful things when you are gazing into someone's eyes. You can still debate the issues. In fact, your discussion will be more constructive and you'll reach resolution more quickly."

Stop, in the Name of Love.

In her counseling experience with couples, Joan Cook has observed that "saying things you later regret" is one of the toughest obstacles to overcome. "Yes, we can forgive, but it's hard to forget words that cut deep. I teach couples to stop themselves from saying things they'll regret. If you realize, mid-sentence, that you are saying something hurtful, just stop. Stop yourself before you get to the last word.

"Your partner might say something like, 'Go ahead, finish. What were you going to say?' Don't give in to temporary curiosity. Instead, say, 'I decided not to say it, because it would have been hurtful. I love you and don't want to hurt you.' Discipline yourself to hear what you, yourself, are saying. Eventually, you'll learn to stop yourself before you get started."

Put Your Spouse First.

We could eliminate ninety percent of conflict if we made it our goal to give, rather than to take. Imagine how wonderful your marriage would be if you both took an attitude that said, "I want to make your life and your job easier. I want to help you in any way I can." As the Bible says, "Each of you should look not only to your own interests, but also to the interests of others" (Phil. 2:4). In the words of Jesus, "So in everything, do to others what you would have them do to you, for this sums up the Law and the Prophets" (Matt. 7:12).

Pray for and With Your Spouse.

We have found one of the most effective ways to improve our communication with each other is through communicating with our Heavenly Father. Each morning, Donna goes on her "prayer walk" through our neighborhood. She has an ever-changing list of items to pray for, but always at the top of the list is Cameron and Leah. As she passes the homes of neighbors we know, she prays for each family. Cameron is the real prayer warrior in our family, though. When he wakes up each morning, he goes directly to his knees to pray. And he continually prays for our family throughout the day.

When you actively pray that God will bring about the very best in someone's life, it's only natural for Him to suggest ways He wants to use you in that process. He often impresses upon your heart words of encouragement or wisdom that you can pass along to your mate.

Also, praying for someone forces you to be in touch with his or her needs. Otherwise, you won't have much to pray about. Knowing your partner's deepest needs will only enhance your communication.

We know of many couples who pray together each night before going to sleep. Earlier in our marriage, we were more consistent about praying as a couple and it definitely enhanced our communication *and* our marriage. Now that we have Leah, we pray together as a family. Unfortunately, we cannot pray very in-depth with a five-year-old. (Although she sure surprises us sometimes!) If you have not prayed consistently for your mate in the past, try it. If you can find a time to also pray with your mate, so much the better. You will be absolutely amazed what a difference it can make.

For Reflection and Discussion

1. Which one of you is more like the Questioner?_____
2. Which one is more like the Spokesperson?_____
3. Can you think of a recent situation where the Questioner/
Spokesperson conflict created a major problem in your business? (Or your marriage?)

_____

_____

_____

4. For the Questioner: what are some specific changes you
plan to make in the way you ask questions of your mate?

_____

_____

_____

5. For the Spokesperson: what are some specific changes you
plan to make in the way you respond to your mate's questions?

_____

_____

_____

6. If you think it will be helpful, make a copy of the list of Fair
and Unfair Questions. Refer to it the next time you think your
partner is asking unfair questions.
7. Discuss whether or not both of you are totally committed

to resolving conflicts in a win-win fashion. Don't settle for "lip service"; look at the record. Does your communication over the last year (five, ten, fifteen years) demonstrate that commitment? Or do you need to make some changes?

_____

_____

_____

8. Are you willing to make a pact with your mate that you will "keep talking until you reach agreement?" Will you make that the absolute rule in your business and personal lives? Make a list of the unchanging issues you are in full agreement on.

We Agree That:

(1) _____

(2) _____

(3) _____

(4) _____

(5) _____

(6) _____

(7) _____

(8) _____

(9) _____

(10) _____

9. Here's a communication-enhancing exercise for you. Pick an issue (political, social, religious) that you know you disagree on and both feel strongly about. Then debate it as passionately as you can. But do it like this: First, the wife (ladies first, of course) states her case as passionately as she can while the husband takes notes. Then, the husband states his case with equal vigor. Now it's time for a full-fledged debate.

One change: the wife must advocate the husband's position and vice versa.

10. Exercise #2. Remember your most romantic date. Write down everything you can remember about it. Now reenact that night as accurately as you possibly can. If you were in Hawaii for your honeymoon and now you're buried under twenty feet of snow in the Rocky Mountains, you'll have to be very creative. That's okay. It may even make the evening more romantic. See for yourself whether or not *acting* in a loving way makes you *feel* loving.

11. Exercise #3. Depending upon how often you fight (ha-ha), you may be able to do this exercise *for real* before the day is done. Otherwise, you can either wait for the next fight to crop up or *invent* a fight just for a good practice session. Sit knee-to-knee, as was described in the chapter, have your battle, then discuss any differences you noticed between your *usual* fights and fighting the knee-to-knee way.

12. Pray for your mate daily. Then, arrange a time when you and your spouse can pray together, daily or weekly.

10
When SHE's Joining the Firm: Do's and Don'ts

ERNIE AND JUDY MORENO met through their banker. He was borrowing money for his business and she was borrowing money to purchase additional investment property. The banker noticed the pair—both in their later years (Ernie is now 67; Judy is 59)—were remarkably similar and decided to play matchmaker. She said to them, "You are both workaholics. You're both free enterprisers. You've already raised your own children. You two should meet!" They met and you can guess the rest.

Judy continued pursuing her career in real estate, while Ernie operated "Ernie's Autobody: Repair and Painting with a Touch of Classic, since 1965." Judy recalls, "He kept asking me to join his business and I kept saying, 'Why would I want to do a thing like that?'" The answer came a few months later when Judy was laid off.

"I agreed to keep his books at home and quickly discovered they were off by $7,000. So I started asking questions: 'What's that secretary doing all day? Why are you paying that guy so much money to push a broom around? Why are you paying a CPA?' He had all kinds of expenses that could be eliminated. Ernie had been in business since 1965, and suddenly I started saving him a lot of money. Once I got the front office in order, I started looking at the shop."

Well, he asked her to join the firm and she did with a vengeance. "I did graphs using Lotus 1–2–3 spreadsheets to show him exactly what was going on in the business. He began to see with his own eyes that he was working many more hours than he needed to and was earning far less than he deserved. He knew the work side, but he didn't know the business side. All these years, he had been making money, but he never really made a profit. There's a big difference between the two."

Judy was shocked to discover he was buying $100 worth of tools every month. "Are they walking out of here?" she asked in true question style! "Do they have legs?" She decided to lay out some bait and sure enough, she caught one of his employees stealing a $200 tool. His nine employees also stole from him by not delivering a full day's work for a full day's pay. "They came and went as they pleased," she recalls. "That really bothered me because I was working day and night, but Ernie insisted he couldn't afford to pay me."

Naturally, the employees did not like Judy! However, they soon had no choice; they had to follow her or leave because Ernie needed to devote all of his energy to the battle of his life: the battle against cancer. One by one, the employees left, but Judy found more reliable replacements. Today, she runs the entire operation with a leaner, meaner staff of four. She has fought hard (*very hard*) for better discounts from suppliers and for higher quality workmanship from independent contractors. It's been an uphill battle for Judy in a male-dominated business. Thanks to her efforts, Ernie's Autobody Shop is now quite profitable. In January 1995, it legally became *her* autobody shop. Ernie wouldn't have it any other way.

Should She Join the Firm?

As you can tell from the battle waged over Ernie's Autobody Shop, it's not always easy for a woman to join a business started by her husband. In fact, when we asked couples what advice they would give to a wife who wants to join her husband's business, the vast majority simply said, "Don't do it!" And we said, "Very funny, wise guys, how about a real answer?" This ought to scare those of you who think you want to work together: that *was* their real answer! This chapter outlines some specific guidelines to keep in mind when the wife wants to join a business started by the husband.

Make Sure There Is a Role That She Has the Desire, Skill, and Experience to Fulfill

It is not enough for the husband to feel overworked and desperately in need of help—any help. In order for the wife to become a genuine partner, there needs to be a specific role that she is qualified to fulfill. That doesn't mean the husband should require a typed resumé. However, a formal job description is definitely in order. More to the point: the job description must be written *before* the wife comes on board. If the company needs an accountant and your wife flunked math, she is the wrong person for the job. She may be willing, she may be smart, but if she is not the right candidate, don't hire her.

Write Out Procedures in Advance

We know you love each other, but your marriage may not survive the first week if the experienced partner has to verbally explain everything. Instead, the husband must invest the time to prepare written directives, wherever possible. He may not know *how* the job should be done (which is probably for the best), but he needs to have a clear idea of what needs to be done and when. As a general rule, written instructions work better than verbal orders.

Accept That Your Spouse Will Handle Things Differently Than You Would

Your wife is not like you. That's why you married her, remember? The husband has to accept that his wife is going to handle things differently. Those things that can only be done *one right way* are the exceptions. Ninety-nine percent of the tasks you do every day could be done just as effectively using a very different approach. Be humble enough to admit that your wife's way might be even better than yours, and when her way yields improved results, be gracious enough to give her the credit she deserves.

Provide Her With Her Own Workspace

Providing your wife with her own workspace is also vitally important. It communicates an important message to her, your clients, and especially your employees, if you have any. It says, "My wife is not here to window dress or to avoid shopping. She has joined the firm because she has an important contribution to make, and in order to fulfill her duties, she needs her own space."

Give Her Specific Responsibility and the Authority to Get It Done

In keeping with the important role your wife will fulfill, give her all of the responsibility and authority she needs to get the job done. This is particularly important if you have employees. If you undercut your wife's authority or tolerate employees who disrespect her, the person you are undermining is *you*; the success you are sabotaging is your own. Do not second-guess your wife. Give her freedom to make her own decisions within her designated areas and to handle any consequences that result. She is certain to make mistakes, but that's part of the learning process that all new business owners must go through. She will be a stronger partner because of the tough lessons she learns.

Notify Clients and Vendors

When your wife joins the firm, let people know about it. Send out a press release to the media and a letter to all of your clients and vendors. Stress your wife's professional credentials and the benefits of having her on the team. Build her up in the eyes of others, so they will give her the benefit of the doubt as she seeks to learn the ropes.

Pay Her a Set Salary

You might be tempted to think, *I'll pay her what I can, when I can. After all, the money is all going to the same place. What's the difference?* R-E-S-P-E-C-T. We cannot overemphasize this, because it is the lifeblood of your business survival. Would you expect your wife to work for someone else in return for occasional and unpredictable paychecks? Of course not. Should you demonstrate more respect to your wife than would a total stranger? *Yes.* Determine what your wife's credentials and contribution warrant and pay her accordingly.

That's not to say you won't face lean times, especially in the beginning, or that your wife won't have to forego a paycheck when business takes a nose dive, which it sometimes will. However, your goal should be a steady paycheck for *both* husband and wife. Far too many self-employed people neglect this basic business practice; they work for slave wages or no wages at all. Listen, if your business cannot yield a steady paycheck after the first year or two in business, find another business or go back to working for a corporation. You deserve to get paid for your efforts. If you refuse to pay yourself, then find someone who *will* pay you.

Set Specific Working Hours

"We love each other, so we'll just work it out as we go along." Ha, ha. Unless you are very careful, you will have one of two very serious problems. Problem Number One: your wife's idea of a day's work falls far short of your expectations and you begin to resent her. Problem Number Two: your wife turns into a workaholic and becomes a frightening shadow of the woman you once fell in love with. Don't fall into the expectations gap: spell out her working hours from day one. Yes, there will be emergencies that require overtime. Yes, she'll have other priorities that demand time away from the office. But, by and large, professionalism and mutual respect demand that both partners commit to specific working hours. Get it right from the start and you'll save yourselves a great deal of heartache and conflict.

For Reflection and Discussion

For the Husband Whose Wife Wants to Join the Firm:

1. Why do you think your wife should join the firm? Be sure to include the specific skills and experiences she brings to the job.

_____

_____

_____

_____

2. Write a procedures manual covering the fundamentals of operating your business. This may seem like a waste of time, but it is not. If you were to become incapacitated tomorrow, would you want your wife to be able to continue running the business? If the answer is yes, then you need a procedures manual. Do you want your business to grow? Do you want to delegate some of the work to others? Then you need a procedures manual. Also, the discipline of writing down the procedures is a revealing and helpful exercise in itself. Just do it!
3. Anticipate some things you suspect your wife will handle differently. How do you think you will react? Ideally, how *should you react*?

_____

_____

_____

_____

4. What arrangements will you need to make to provide your wife with her own workspace?

_____

_____

_____

_____

5. Draft a letter to your clients and vendors notifying them that your wife is joining the firm.
6. Discuss working hours with your wife.
7. How much money do you think a person with your wife's credentials should be paid to fulfill the job you have in mind?

_____

8. Realistically, how much can you afford to pay her?_____

_____

9. If there is a significant discrepancy between the two salaries, be sure to discuss this with your wife.

For the Wife Who Thinks She Wants to Join the Firm:

1. Why do you want to join the firm?

_____

_____

_____

2. What changes do you expect to make to your husband's current business practice? Why?

_____

_____

_____

_____

3. Review your husband's answers to the questions preceding these. Discuss any differences that become apparent.

11
When HE's Joining the Firm: Do's and Don'ts

WHEN GERA WITTE LAUNCHED Paragon Communications in February of 1989, her goal was to stay involved in challenging work on a part-time basis while raising her son. That modest beginning has since grown into a $400,000 per year business, employing Gera and her husband, Jim. They have even managed to involve their two sons, ages seven and four.

"From the very beginning, we talked about the possibility of Jim joining me at some point. He had decided early on in his career that he wanted to start his own business someday. It was always in the back of our minds that we might work together," recalls Gera.

"I think Jim was a little surprised how well my business was going. That gave him the extra push he needed to strike out on his own. Finally, about three years after I started the business, Jim set the date when he would leave his job." For several months before he officially joined the business, Jim was laying the groundwork. As a result, on his first day in the home office he had appointments all day with new clients. "The transition went very smoothly," the couple recalls.

During evenings and weekends, Jim refinished the basement and converted it into a large open office. "We wanted to make sure we had enough room to accommodate both of us comfortably. We both need our space," explains Jim. He also bought new equipment, came up with a new business name, The W Group, and had stationery printed.

Most importantly, the Wittes decided exactly what role each of them would play based on their respective strengths. "Jim is the creative genius and graphic designer. I provide copywriting, project management, and consulting services. We each have accounts that we are primarily responsible for, but we help each other with specific tasks. If Jim is doing a project that requires copywriting, I do it. If one of my clients needs graphic design, Jim is responsible for that part of the project."

Jim and Gera prepare their own proposals and bill their clients individually. Jim is the technology support person, while Gera handles bookkeeping, payables, and receivables. To hold each other accountable, they schedule production meetings to discuss what work they have to do and what each partner has to contribute. They have a wipe-off marker board where they each list projects with which they need help.

Jim and Gera also attended to family matters before Jim joined the firm. "We settled into a house that would hold us for many years. We made sure our cars were in good shape for the next few years. We shopped around for our own health insurance. We didn't want to have any big expenditures sneak up on us. We talked a lot about how we wanted to handle child care and came up with an arrangement we both feel good about."

The next step was to send an announcement to all of Gera's customers informing them of the new partnership and the new services they could provide. Initially, Gera had focused on copywriting. With Jim on board, she could now offer design services and marketing communications. In short, it became a full-fledged advertising agency.

"We really emphasized the benefits Jim could offer the customers. Most of them already knew that Jim was a graphic designer working with another ad agency. So it came as no surprise when he joined the firm." Gera says her customers took the transition in stride. Today, all of Gera's initial customers use the additional services offered through Jim.

Determining Who's the BOSS

Unfortunately, the transition is not always as smooth as it was for the Wittes. When a husband decides to join the company his wife launched, all the rules listed in the previous chapter apply. In addition, there's the nagging question about "who's the boss?" Whether we like it or not, a great many outsiders will assume that the husband will take the helm. Even in those instances where the wife started the company and continues to run the business, some people believe she is just a figurehead. The couple must learn to manage the perceptions of clients, vendors, and employees. Again, following all of the suggestions provided in the previous chapter should help you achieve a smooth transition.

Can a Christian Wife Be the Boss?

For those of us who live according to Christian principles, the idea of the wife as the boss can cause a few additional problems. That's because the Bible clearly teaches that the husband is the head of the household. What are the implications of that teaching for a couple-owned business? We have heard many Christian business leaders say that the husband must be the head of the business and the wife must take a subservient role. We want to share with you the conclusions we have come to in our own hearts and minds. However, we are not claiming this is the *one true way*. It's just what works for us.

After much prayer and some very lively debates, we have decided the solution lies in our recognition and acceptance of the way God has created us. We are absolutely convinced that Christian marriages are made in heaven. We also believe that God creates each of us with a unique set of talents and temperaments with which we are to fulfill a very specific purpose in this world. We further believe that God brings together couples to fulfill specific tasks.

Now, please follow us carefully on the next part. If *God* brings together an Executive wife and an Operations husband and leads them to start a business, yet *we* insist that the husband must always serve as the Executive and that the wife must always serve as the Operations Partner . . . where do we think God made the mistake? Did He make a mistake when He fashioned the wife? The husband? Was the marriage a mismatch from the beginning? Was God confused when He laid it on their hearts to go into business together? What do you think? Should we help God out by pretending to be someone other than the person He created us to be? Some would say yes.

We have struggled with this issue in our own marriage because I (Donna) am clearly gifted as the Executive/Promoter, while Cameron is obviously the Operations/Financial Partner. Should we deceive people by labeling Cameron the president? Would that make us appear more spiritual to outsiders? Or should we rejoice in the unique gifts God has given to each of us? Should we be thankful that, in combination, we have everything we need to run a successful business? We believe honesty is the best policy.

We are in no way denying the biblical mandate that the husband is the head of the home. However, we don't believe the Bible indicates the husband must also be president of the family business. More to the point, who is to say that a company president is a more valuable human being than the operations manager who quietly gets the job done. Cameron *is* the head of our household. Donna's brother, Dan, lived with us for about a year. As he was preparing to move out on his own, we were curious to hear his perceptions about our marriage. Guess what he said? "Donna may do a lot of clucking, but Cameron rules the roost."

When we began conducting interviews for this book, we were amazed to discover the number of couples who were exactly like us. In fact, we found very few instances where the husband started the business—which is not to say those couples don't exist. For the most part, the couples started the business simultaneously. The second most common scenario was the husband joining the wife.

What If He Is the Right Man for the Job?

In some cases, the husband may very well be the right person to run the business even though the wife launched it. For example, she may be a great Promoter who attracts business, but may lack the management skills and training needed to take the business to higher levels of growth. Rather than engaging in turf wars or personality conflicts, sit down and evaluate who is better suited to lead the company into the future. If the husband is the right man for the job, then so be it. The wife should be more committed to the success of the business and the happiness of her marriage than she is to an ego trip about being the boss.

In this case, *before* the husband comes on board, the couple should arrange a timetable for the gradual transfer of power. The wife should determine where her talents can achieve the most good and focus her energy there. Meanwhile, she can turn over an increasing share of the decision-making and administrative issues to her husband.

If there are employees involved, the matter will have to be handled with great diplomacy. There are two things that should never be tolerated from employees: disrespect and gamesmanship. Employees must continue to respect the wife as the founder of the company and must also respect the husband as their new boss. Most important, do not allow your employees to pull the old childhood power-play routine. You know, Dad says no, so you go to Mom for a second opinion. Do not tolerate this behavior. If you ignore it, it will destroy your business and possibly even your marriage.

What About Usurpers?

We're not naming names, but believe us, it happens all the time. We have seen it happen before our very eyes. The husband joins the business and promptly takes over. In the beginning it was *her* business. Within a month it becomes *our* business, and before you know it, the husband is calling it *my* business and treating his wife like a second-class citizen.

Maybe we're naive, but we can't imagine that this type of behavior suddenly comes out of nowhere. People who like to grab for power are *always* grabbing for power. Ladies, listen up! If your husband consistently overrules you in your personal relationship, don't expect any better treatment on the job. If you want to keep the reins of your business in hand, you had better think long and hard about inviting your husband to join the company. Unless, of course, you *want* him to take control, in which case, reread the previous section.

Speaking personally, the best business decision I (Donna) ever made was to invite my husband to join my company. His insight and advice are always on target. And many of our best times have come through our working together. We trust it will be the same for you.

For Reflection and Discussion

For the Wife Whose Husband Wants to Join the Firm:

1. Why do you think your husband should join the firm? Be sure to include the specific skills and experiences he brings to the company.

_____

_____

_____

_____

2. What role will your husband fulfill? Will he take over the leadership of the company or will you continue as the boss? Think through and discuss the various issues raised in the chapter.

_____

_____

_____

3. Write a procedures manual covering the fundamentals of operating your business. (See comments in previous chapter.)
4. Anticipate some things you suspect your husband will handle differently. How can you plan ahead to respond appropriately?

_____

_____

_____

_____

5. What arrangements will you need to make to provide your husband with his own workspace?

_____

_____

_____

6. Draft a letter to your clients and vendors, notifying them that your husband is joining the firm. Be sure to clearly explain his role.

7. Discuss working hours with your husband.

8. What do you think someone with your husband's credentials should be paid to fulfill the job you have in mind?_____

_____

9. Realistically, how much can you afford to pay him?_____

_____

10. If there is a significant discrepancy between the two salaries, be sure to discuss this with your husband.

For the Husband Who Wants to Join His Wife:

1. Why do you want to join the firm?

_____

_____

_____

_____

2. What changes do you expect to make to your wife's current business practice? Why?

_____

_____

_____

_____

3. Are you comfortable with the role your wife has in mind for you to fulfill? If your wife will continue to be the boss, can you keep your "male ego" in check? Now is the time to deal honestly with these issues.

_____

_____

_____

_____

4. Review your wife's answers to the preceding questions. Discuss any differences that become apparent.

PART FOUR

MANAGING THE BUSINESS

12
Managing for Efficiency and Effectiveness

LIKE MOST YOUNG COUPLES, Jim and Jill Mapstead, owners of Accurate Engraving and parents of two preschool children, constantly strive to balance the competing demands of family and career. In addition to their storefront, Jill maintains an office at home, complete with a Macintosh computer, a printer, a fax machine, and a floor-to-ceiling bookshelf. Jill uses her home office to run two part-time businesses: a technical writing service and a direct sales distributorship. If that doesn't sound like enough work, Jill is the Secretary of a very active chapter of the National Association of Women Business Owners (NAWBO).

So how does she manage three different businesses, a family, and a demanding volunteer position? "I color-code everything," she says. "I'm a firm believer in 'divide and conquer,' so I keep everything separate. If I look at the whole picture, it's overwhelming. Instead, I take it a task at a time and blow right through it. It's like crashing through the Berlin Wall. Of course it seems impossible, but when it's done, I know I've accomplished something important."

In keeping with the Mapsteads divide-and-conquer strategy, the responsibilities at the office are carefully

146

segregated. "Jim handles all of the customer contacts— I probably wouldn't know half our customers if they were staring me in the face. Jim is in full charge of the front office; I rarely even go up there." Meanwhile, Jill handles all of the paperwork (billing, accounting) in the back room.

Efficiency Versus Effectiveness

Most of us can't help feeling a bit envious of people like Jill Mapstead. You know, those incredibly organized people who seem to thrive on five hours of sleep per night. The kind of people who have a place for everything and just *love* keeping everything in its place. The fact is, most of us are not naturally that efficient. We can improve, but we'll probably never become efficiency experts. Nevertheless, we can be highly effective.

What's the difference between efficiency and effectiveness? Efficiency is doing things right; effectiveness is doing the right things. Some of the most efficient people we know lead very ineffective lives. That's because they channel their considerable energies into mundane tasks which have no lasting consequence. We knew a woman who rearranged her furniture every single week. She worked hard and was extremely efficient, but did she accomplish anything of real value? It's doubtful. Efficiency is wonderful, provided it is channeled toward worthy goals.

That's where effectiveness comes in. You can expend far less time and energy, yet accomplish more if you focus on the things that matter most. However, before you can channel your efforts effectively, you must first identify your goal.

Business Goal-Setting

Ideally, you prepared long-range goals back in Chapter 5, "Your Business Plan." If not, go back now and work through the exercises provided. Once you have a completed Business Plan, break it down even further. Explore the question: "In view of this Business Plan, what specific goals do we have for the next ten years? The next five years? This year?" Put those one-, five-, and ten-year goals in writing. Then refer to them frequently, asking yourselves: "In view of these goals, what should we do this month? This week? This morning? Is the work we're doing right now the most effective use of our time and energy?"

Here is a fictitious illustration showing why it is so important to continually monitor your efforts for effectiveness: imagine that you and your beloved spouse set out on a journey from New York to San Francisco. With your ultimate destination in view, you hop in the car and head west. So far, so good. Two weeks later, you arrive at the end of the road: the Pacific Ocean. You have achieved your goal, right? Actually, no. You see, you have arrived in San Diego.

You worked hard. You invested time and money. You made sacrifices. You were headed in the right general direction. So where did you go wrong? *You neglected to check the map to make sure you stayed on the right road.* Wouldn't it have been far better to monitor your progress along the journey, rather than waiting until you arrived at the final destination, only to discover you had made a wrong turn many miles back?

Weekly Evaluation

When we conduct seminars around the country, we offer the participants a money-back guarantee if they will take up the following challenge: every week, for the next six months, set aside time to reflect upon the following questions:

1. Which of my business and personal goals did I pursue this week?
2. Which of my goals did I fail to pursue?

3. Was I effective or merely efficient?
4. Am I devoting an appropriate amount of time to: my business, my marriage, my family, my personal development? Or do I need to strive for a better balance?
5. What specific goals do I have for the coming week?

A Friday or Sunday afternoon would be an excellent time for this exercise, which will take fifteen to thirty minutes. Yet it will make a world of difference when you come to the end of your journey. It's the difference between San Francisco and San Diego! If you faithfully take time to reflect for the next six months and it doesn't *absolutely revolutionize* the way you live, write to us and we'll refund you the price of this book. We know it works.

Applying the 80/20 Rule

Remember the battle cry for women in the 1980s: "We can have it all"? Other than a handful of superwomen, most of us discovered it simply wasn't true. You can't have it all, but you can have those things you are truly committed to having. You can have those things for which you are willing to sacrifice. The way to have the things you really want—in life and in business, for men and for women—is to apply the 80/20 Rule.

The 80/20 Rule, also known as the Paretto Principal, is named after an Italian economist who noted that 80% of any return is usually derived from 20% of the investment. It's one of those mysteries of the universe that seems to fly in the face of rational analysis. For example, 20% of any sales force typically generates the most business. Twenty percent of products in any given store generally accounts for 80% of the sales. You'll probably discover that 20% of your clients yields 80% of your profits.

You can either spend your life trying to disprove the 80/20 Rule, or you can use it as a powerful tool to increase your effectiveness. We hope you'll choose the latter. Take the time to determine the 20% of your time, effort, clients, products, that yields the 80% return. Everything else—the remaining 80% that yields only 20%—should be streamlined, delegated, or eliminated.

Streamline

Many everyday activities can and should be streamlined, that is, simplified and made more manageable. The objective of streamlining is this: to modify the amount of time required for an activity *until it accurately reflects the true importance of the task.* Cooking provides a simple illustration. Eating is important, but is it important enough to consume countless hours and endless hassle each week? Does cooking have to be such an onerous, energy-draining task? Absolutely not! A little streamlining will do the trick.

Rather than flying into a frenzy each night around 5:30 P.M., plan to cook once a week. Then, after a hard day's work, it's just freezer to microwave. A few years ago, Mimi Wilson and Mary Beth Lagerborg released a book called *Once-a-Month Cooking.* It became an instant bestseller. Last time I checked with the publisher, it had sold over 200,000 copies. By the way, an added advantage of streamlining is that it can become the basis for an excellent business. If you come up with a viable strategy for streamlining an activity—in other words, you develop a specific solution to a common problem—you've hit upon the magic success formula we discussed back in Chapter 5. That's exactly what Mimi and Mary Beth did.

The home office offers another excellent example. Once upon a time in the 1980s, some executive got frustrated with his five-hour daily commute. (He was probably from California.) He just knew he could use those hours more effectively elsewhere. He decided to streamline his commute. He started working at home on Fridays; that freed up an extra five hours per week. It felt so good, he worked at home two days per week. He was saving ten hours per week and, to his utter amazement, forty hours per month. He was so overjoyed, he streamlined his commute from twenty-five hours per week to three minutes per week and gave up the corporate office forever. And he lived happily ever after. (Well, it probably went something like that!)

Any time-consuming tasks—espccially those of the mundane variety—are prime candidates for the streamlining process. A great way to uncover activities that should be streamlined is to conduct a Time Inventory. Here's how it works: photocopy the Time Inventory chart found at the end of this chapter. For one week, carry the chart with you and jot down how you spend the better part of each half hour (both at work and at home). Try to follow your normal routine as much as possible so you will get an accurate reading on where your time is spent.

At the end of the week, analyze how effectively you invested your time. Determine which activities need to be streamlined and look for areas that can be delegated or eliminated altogether.

Delegate

Many entrepreneurs fall into the trap of continuing to do it all even when they no longer have to do so. During the lean, early years, entrepreneurs *have* to do everything just to survive. They have to be secretary, receptionist, accountant, errand boy, and executive all rolled into one. At some point, you need to release the more mundane activities and free yourself up to do those things only you can do. In other words, you need to delegate. It may mean hiring a secretary or using a secretarial service. It may mean turning your financials over to a bookkeeper or CPA. Or it may simply involve training your spouse or children to handle routine tasks.

Unfortunately, letting go of any part of your "baby" is hard. It is especially difficult for the Executive Partner and the Financial Partner (refer to Chapter 7, "Which

Type of Partner Are You?") The Executive tends to be a "control freak" and can't bear to let the work out of his sight, while the Financial whiz tends to get bogged down in perfectionism, convinced that his way is the *only* way and no one else can do it as well as he. However, if you want your business to grow and prosper, delegating is a vital first step on the journey. What do *you* need to delegate?

Eliminate

Some things we do are simply a waste of time, either because they add nothing to the quality of our lives or because they actually diminish it. An example from Donna's business was her involvement in public relations. When we conducted an 80/20 analysis of Donna's business, we realized that 80% of her profits came from writing and speaking. On the other hand, we noted that she devoted 80% of her time and emotional energy to her public relations clients who yielded only a small percentage of her income. (Dare we say it? About 20%!) As a result, Donna completely eliminated her public relations business. She has had far fewer headaches while earning more money. What can you eliminate from your business? From your life?

Office Supply Sources

Okay, you have streamlined, delegated, and eliminated. What else can you do to increase your effectiveness? Outfit your business for success. We have been amazed by the productivity-enhancing supplies available for today's entrepreneur or business owner. Some items which we now consider indispensable include: computer (obviously!), glare screen, laser printer, telephone headset, wipe-off white board, postage scale and meter, ergonomically-correct chairs, and a cassette player stocked with uplifting music.

You already know about the Most Dangerous Place in America: OfficeMax. But to add a little more danger to your life, here's a list of companies that supply the goodies through the mail.

Day-Timers, Inc.
One Day-Timer Plaza
Allentown, PA 18195
215–266–9000
Preprinted personal organizers and planners.

Global Computer Supplies
11 Harbor Park Drive
Port Washington, NY 11050
800–845–6225
Computers, computer supplies, office furniture.

Hello Direct
5884 Eden Park Place
San Jose, CA 95138
800–444–3556
Telephone productivity tools including headsets—an absolute must for anyone who spends time on the phone. One of the smartest investments we ever made.

NEBS Computer Forms and Software
500 Main Street
Groton, MA 01471
800–225–9550
Custom-order computer forms, stationery, and labels.

PaperAccess
23 W. 18th Street
New York, NY 10011
800–727–3701
Great looking papers. Call for free catalog.

Paper Direct
205 Chubb Avenue
Lyndhurst, NJ 07071
800–272–7377.
Great looking desk-top publishing paper, plus software design templates that make looking professional easy.

Penny-Wise Office Products
4350 Kenilworth Avenue
Edmonston, MD 20781
800–942–3311
Mail-order office supplies at discount prices. Additional discounts if you order via computer.

Pitney Bowes
40 Lindeman Drive
Trumbull, CT 06611
800–672–6937
Postage meters.

Quill Corporation
100 Schelter Road
Lincolnshire, IL 60069
717–272–6100
Office supplies via the mail. Great prices.

For Reflection and Discussion

1. Time Inventory Exercise[1]

To use the Time Inventory, list up to thirty activities you frequently do each day, both on the job and around the house. Typical activities might include: sales, marketing, billing, phone calls, travel time, TV, exercise, etc. Once your numbering system is worked out, you can simply write the appropriate number in the corresponding time slot. It's easier to plug in numbers than write out the activities each time. This also makes it easier to calculate your total hours for each activity at the end of the week.

2. Time Inventory Evaluation

Prior to calculating your totals in each category, take a moment to assign a value to each. For example, you might decide that marketing deserves ten hours per week, while billing deserves only three hours per week. Then review the chart to determine exactly how many hours you actually spent on each activity and compare the two numbers. You may find it quite disconcerting to discover where your time goes. Don't get down on yourself, but rather determine to take action. Decide specifically which activities you should streamline, delegate, or eliminate. And finally, determine exactly *how* to implement your decisions to streamline, delegate, and eliminate. Take heart. Identifying the problem is half the solution. If both husband and wife complete this activity, com-

---

[1]Adapted from *Working Smart*, by Michael LeBoeuf (McGraw Hill, 1979).

pare notes and offer each other constructive feedback and ideas for positive change.

3. Weekly Evaluation Worksheet

On the following page, you will find a copy of the Weekly Evaluation Worksheet. Make several dozen copies and complete one each week for the next six months.

WEEKLY EVALUATION WORKSHEET

1. Which of my business and personal goals did I pursue this week?

_____

_____

_____

_____

2. Which of my goals did I fail to pursue?

_____

_____

3. Was I effective or merely efficient?

_____

_____

4. Am I devoting an appropriate amount of time to: my business, my marriage, my family, my personal development? Or do I need to strive for a better balance?

_____

_____

_____

_____

5. What specific goals do I have for the coming week?

_____

_____

_____

_____

TIME INVENTORY EVALUATION

Activity	Est. Hours	Actual Hours	Stream-line (√)	Dele-gate(√)	Elimi-nate (√)
1.					
2.					
3.					
4.					
5.					
6.					
7.					
8.					
9.					
10.					
11.					
12.					
13.					
14.					
15.					
16.					
17.					
18.					
19.					
20.					
21.					
22.					
23.					
24.					
25.					
26.					
27.					
28.					
29.					
30.					

TIME INVENTORY CHART

Time	Sunday	Monday	Tuesday
5:00			
6:00			
7:00			
8:00			
9:00			
10:00			
11:00			
12:00			
1:00			
2:00			
3:00			
4:00			
5:00			
6:00			
7:00			
8:00			
9:00			
10:00			

Wednesday	Thursday	Friday	Saturday

13
Accountability Without Nagging or Dominating

IN CHAPTERS 10 AND 11, we discussed the importance of respecting each other enough to *not* interfere. Yet one of the major advantages of having a business partner is the accountability it provides. Knowing you are responsible to another person can motivate you to work, especially when you don't have any specific deadlines to meet. Unfortunately, when a husband and wife live and work together, the line between holding each other accountable and nagging or dominating can become blurred.

"My husband, David, is an absolute perfectionist. Not me. I'll work on something until it's good enough, and then I'll quit," says author and professional speaker, Sue Ellen Allen. "He will keep telling me to rework it or refine it when I really don't want to." Sue Ellen also grew weary of David's constant reminders. "When you've been reminded for the tenth time, you don't want to hear it again."

David came up with a solution that satisfied both of them—it satisfied his need to feel he had taken action on something and her need not to hear verbal reminders. "David found two old shoe boxes and painted them a beautiful emerald green [their official company color].

Then he labeled one for Sue Ellen and one for David. "Now whenever we think of something the other person should do or follow-up on, we write a note and place it in the box."

Sue Ellen says this system works especially well for issues that are not urgent but yet are important enough to warrant her attention at some point in the future. It also allows the pair to communicate without interrupting each other. That's especially important for them because Sue Ellen is a poet and a very creative person. If David were to burst in during one of her highly creative moments, wanting to know whether or not she had bought postage stamps, it would be extremely frustrating and counterproductive.

At the end of the day, David and Sue Ellen sit down and empty out their boxes. "It works really well and gives us a chance to review what we accomplished today and what we need to do tomorrow," says Sue Ellen. "The quality of our communication is much better at this point, because we've both put behind us the concerns of the day and are ready to concentrate on the contents of our boxes."

Actions Speak Louder Than Words

We were amazed at how many couples expressed the view that there is no way to hold your partner accountable. Most believed both partners had to be self-motivated. "I'm not sure there is a way for a couple to hold each other accountable without a situation deteriorating into a power struggle," says Bill Black, who operates Beyond Words, Inc., a desktop publishing firm, with his wife, Diane. "Supposedly you have two mature adults who are capable of recognizing each other's weaknesses and strengths. And you are motivated enough to want to build on the strengths that each brings to the partnership." He warns, "If a husband and wife aren't totally committed to bringing out the best in each other, they probably shouldn't be working together anyway." The Blacks' motto is: "There is no limit to what you can accomplish if you don't care who gets the credit."

Naomi Rhode, of SmartPractice, a professional speaking and consulting business, puts it more succinctly: "It's not my job to motivate him and it's not his job to motivate me. I let him worry about holding up his end of the bargain, and I worry about mine."

Despite the consensus among our interviewees that it *can't be done*, we want to offer you some Do's and Don'ts which might help. Try a few of these ideas. If they work for you, great; if not, you'll be all the wiser.

Do's

1. *Hold Monday morning staff meetings.* It doesn't have to be a long, formal meeting, but if you want it to be effective, then be consistent. Every Monday, perhaps over a cup of coffee, sit down and share with each other what you hope to accomplish by Friday afternoon. Then put it in *writing*, for the reason described below. This is a great way to get focused and geared up for the coming week.

2. *Set written goals that are easy to measure.* If each partner sets specific, measurable goals he or she is committed to achieving, then there is an objective standard against which performance can be measured. For example, if Donna makes a firm commitment to write twenty pages by Friday afternoon, then Cameron is perfectly justified to look her in the eye and say, "Well, let me have a look at those twenty pages." Of course, everyone works differently. When Cameron sets a goal, it's as good as done; he doesn't want or need Donna to remind him.

3. *Reward success.* It's not enough to check up on goals. Once they are achieved, they should be rewarded. You can establish your own reward when you set the goal. Back to the writing example: if Donna writes

twenty pages by Friday afternoon, then Friday night we will go out to dinner at the restaurant of her choice. Or you can choose to reward your partner for an important goal that was achieved. Buy him a new CD to relax and unwind with; surprise your wife with a bouquet of flowers. True, success is its own reward, but a little bonus never hurts.

4. *Encourage each other.* Does this sound like your theme song: "Home, home at the office, where the computer and the fax machine play. Where seldom is heard, an encouraging word, and the skies are just cloudy all day." Try to think, speak, and act positively. We know it's hard when the bills are due and your best client just walked away. But when things go wrong, don't beat each other up. So often, we blame our mate when we're down and talk about shoulda, coulda, woulda. What's the point? If your partner blows it, forgive her and move on. Encourage her to believe she'll close the deal next time.

5. *Pitch in where needed and wanted.* We've talked so much about dividing responsibilities and giving each other room to work that some of you may be thinking, "Does that mean we can't help each other or work on anything as a team?" Not at all. You can and should help your spouse, whenever possible. There is one caveat, though. As Cameron often says, "Help in a helpful way." Some of us have major trouble with that, and when we offer to help, what we really want is to have it done *our way.* If that's the only kind of help you know how to offer, maybe you shouldn't help. However, if your spouse needs and wants your help, roll up your sleeves and get to it.

Don'ts

1. *Treat the business like a hobby.* Nothing is more aggravating to a hard-working entrepreneur than a partner with a cavalier attitude. If you are not willing to carry your share of the load, your spouse would be bet-

ter served by finding someone else who will truly enhance the business. (We're not advocating divorce here, we are trying to *prevent* divorce!)

2. *Treat the business like a god.* Come to think of it, maybe there *is* something more aggravating than a partner with a "hobby" attitude. And that's a partner who treats the business like a god. The success of your business is important, but it's not a matter of life or death. If you give everything you have to the business, what will be left for your marriage? Don't lose perspective or you may lose both your marriage and your business.

3. *Nag.* "Honey, did you? Honey, will you? Honey, could you?" Solomon says, "A nagging wife annoys like constant dripping" (Prov. 19:13, TLB); so does a nagging business partner. If you absolutely can't resist the temptation to "remind" your spouse about his or her responsibilities, at least have the courtesy to put your requests in writing.

4. *Put down.* If you belittle your spouse and shake her confidence with constant put-downs, your business will go down, too. No one can function successfully in a critical environment. If you can't say something positive, don't say anything at all.

5. *Assign blame.* When things go wrong, as they often will, resist the temptation to assign blame. You are in this together and you are in it for the long haul. Does it really matter who is at fault? Will placing blame win back a lost deal? Will it put money in the bank? The truth is, it won't do any good and it might do serious harm. If your partner blew it, he surely knows it and that awareness is "punishment" enough. Don't let the frustration of the moment cause you to say things you'll regret later. Besides, a good leader takes a little more than his share of the blame, a little less than his share of the credit.

6. *Raise the bar or move the target.* You know how this works. Your partner says "write twenty pages by Friday," and the minute you finish the twenty pages, he imme-

diately announces that he wants twenty-five pages. (Yes, that is a true-life example from the Partows!) By establishing your *own* goals and putting them in writing, you can prevent your spouse from trying to raise the bar or move the target on you.

7. *Let things slide, and slide, and slide.* Is there ever a time to speak up? Should you just let your partner roll merrily along the river of life, floating obliviously toward the waterfall of failure? Should you just hold your feelings inside and let them eat away at you? No. If your partner is genuinely failing to live up to his or her commitments (again, those written goals come into play), don't let it slide forever. Virtually all entrepreneurs go through periods of discouragement, especially after facing a major setback. However, if you really love your partner, you can't let him wallow in self-pity or self-recrimination forever. Help him get back on his feet and moving forward toward the goal.

8. *Accept excuses.* With all this talk about "nicey, nice," you probably think the Partows are a pair of wimps. Not on your life. We have a firm "NO EXCUSES" policy around here. It's okay to say, "I blew it, please forgive me," or "I'm sorry I didn't get it right last time, here's what I plan to do differently . . ." Even winners make mistakes, but only losers make excuses. If you want the best for your spouse and your business, don't accept any excuses. Be nice, but don't accept excuses!

Is Accountability Possible?

So, is it possible to hold your spouse accountable without nagging or dominating? We think so! At the end of this chapter, you will have opportunity to review some of the Do's and Don'ts of holding each other accountable. We encourage you to take the time to work through the questions and to develop strategies that will work for you well into the future.

For Reflection and Discussion

1. What do you think of the idea of Monday morning staff meetings? If the idea seems realistic to you, schedule your first one for next Monday and be sure to mark the time and place on your calendars. Perhaps you'll hold these breakfast meetings at a local coffee shop where you can get a fresh perspective for the coming week. Also, brainstorm ideas for topics that should be covered and the format you will follow. Establish guidelines in advance.

_____

_____

_____

_____

_____

2. Each of you should prepare a list of specific goals you would like your partner to hold you accountable to:

HIS GOALS:

This week:

_____   _____

_____   _____

Next 60 days:

_____   _____

_____   _____

This year:

_____   _____

_____   _____

HER GOALS:

This week:

_____   _____

_____   _____

Next 60 days

_____   _____

_____   _____

This Year

_____   _____

_____   _____

3. Recap your five most important goals (can be from any time frame: weekly, monthly, annually) and list an appropriate reward you would like to receive when you achieve it.

HIS GOALS	REWARDS

HER GOALS	REWARDS
_____	_____
_____	_____
_____	_____
_____	_____
_____	_____

4. Let's assume you've done a great job at work this week, and your spouse wants to give you a surprise reward. What kind of rewards would be most rewarding for you? List ten ideas each, ranging from freebies like a back rub, to cheapies like an ice cream cone, all the way to a weekend for two at your favorite Bed & Breakfast or a new boat! (You can dream, can't you?)

HIS IDEA OF A GOOD REWARD

_____

_____

_____

_____

_____

_____

_____

_____

HER IDEA OF A GOOD REWARD

_____

_____

_____

_____

_____

_____

_____

_____

_____

_____

5. We shared with you Cameron's saying, "Help in a helpful way." Discuss what that means to each of you. Can you think of times when your spouse helped in a helpful way? Without getting into the blame game, you might also discuss situations where your spouse's attempts to be helpful were not appreciated. For example, sometimes when people try to help, they become very controlling, condescending, or manipulative. Note any comments or insights below.

_____

_____

_____

_____

_____

6. Which extreme is a greater danger for you: treating the business like a hobby or allowing the business to become a god? Explore why and discuss steps you can take to approach the business in a healthy, balanced way.

HIS ANSWER:

_____

_____

_____

_____

HER ANSWER:

_____

_____

_____

_____

7. Honestly evaluate the quality of your communication. Do either or both of you have a tendency to be negative: nagging, putting down, assigning blame? Realizing how detrimental those activities are, not only to your business but to your marriage, discuss some positive changes you plan to make.

14
Staying Ahead by Staying Innovative

HOW CAN A HUSBAND-WIFE team stay competitive in a world of corporate giants? How can they fight to win in the proverbial David-and-Goliath battle? Innovation! Now that the factory of the Information Age is the human mind, a savvy duo like you two have a better chance than ever. That's because you don't need better (and more expensive) equipment . . . you just need better *ideas*. Thankfully, ideas don't require huge capital investments; they require time and know-how.

Did you know the average person uses less than one-tenth of one percent of his brain power? You can do better than that, and with the help of this chapter, you *will*. "We now know that breakthrough ideas come from the integration of logic and imagination—the merging of left brain (analytical, convergent) and right brain (creative, divergent) thinking," says Chic Thompson, author of *What a Great Idea!* (HarperCollins). "We can transform our minds into idea-generating powerhouses if we learn to operate them at peak efficiency." Innate convergent thinkers, like the Financial Partner, often find that their linear approach is too limiting. They get stuck on the root of an idea and find it difficult to branch out. Naturally divergent thinkers, such as the Executive

Partner, pop out plenty of ideas but find it difficult to backtrack, focus, and bring a single concept to full development.

Here again, the old "opposites attract" formula can work in your favor. By gaining a better understanding of how the mind works and which of you is more suited to the two phases of creative and analytical thinking, you can become a great idea-generating factory.

Identify a Problem Before You Create a Solution

"It just hit me" is probably your explanation for how your business initially came about. But how can you continue to stay innovative? How can you generate fresh ideas to keep your business on the cutting edge? "The best ideas start with a passion to solve a specific problem or to find an answer to a burning question," says Thompson. Simply asking yourself the right questions is a launching pad to problem solving. The world changed forever when the first nomad stopped asking, "How do we get to water?" and asked instead, "How can we get the water to come to us?"

It was sheer frustration that led Phillip Payne of Edmonds, Washington, on a quest for a solution that would eventually evolve into a fruitful business. Twenty years ago, Phillip was a Cambridge University student typing his doctoral dissertation on an IBM Selectric typewriter. "Much of my research was in Hebrew and Greek," recalls the Bible scholar. "It was an extremely painful process because I had to leave blank spaces, then go back and hand-write the foreign lettering. His wife, Nancy, often urged him to write a book based upon his research, but he was hindered because there was no software that handled English, Hebrew, and Greek. "I realized the need for a system that could handle both Roman and non-Roman scripts. The minute I saw the

Macintosh WYSIWYG interface, I knew I'd found my answer," says Phillip.

Within a month, he was printing documents in Greek. Phillip was so elated with his discovery that he wrote to a computer magazine, describing his work. Then, he wrote an article about it in a 1984 issue, and the Paynes's phone started ringing off the hook. Today, Phillip, Nancy, and their three children are all involved in Linguist's Software, which recently topped $600,000 in annual sales.

Ready, Fire, Aim

If you want to generate fresh ideas, "Ready, Fire, Aim" should be your motto. Clearly identify the problem you want to tackle by asking the right questions (Ready). Financial and Operations Partners should play a vital role at this stage. Next, throw out dozens—even hundreds—of possible solutions, from wacky to wonderful, from silly to sublime. That's the Fire stage and is, without question, the Executive Partner's specialty. At least one of these ideas is bound to be good (Aim). The Financial Partner will probably have the analytical skill needed for the Aim, where you narrow down your ideas to the one best solution.

The notebooks of geniuses like Leonardo da Vinci and Albert Einstein are filled with scribbles, doodles, and unconnected thoughts—all evidence of a vigorous Fire stage. Keep that in mind, Mr. Financial Partner, when you start getting impatient with the Executive Partner's never-ending stream of ideas to pursue and projects to undertake.

Where to Find Fuel for Thought

Ideas to fuel the Fire stage can be so simple that people often overlook or dismiss them. "Fuel for great ideas lurks everywhere," says Bill Shephard, director of programs for the Creative Education Foundation in Buffalo, New York. "Newspapers, magazines, and books are filled with idea fodder. So are nature and recreation. Children are infinitely creative and often spark new ideas." He cites a case in point. When Edwin Land took a picture of his young daughter playing at the beach, she asked when she could see it. Land replied that the film had to be developed first. His daughter asked, "Why can't we see the picture now?" That question inspired Land to invent the instant photography technology for the Polaroid Land camera.

The moral, of course, is *listen to your children.* Involve them in the business. Answer their endless litany of questions and don't dismiss even the zaniest of their ideas. Let them challenge why you do things the way you do. And while you are answering them, you may hit upon a great new idea or a whole new direction for your business.

Create a Brain-Nourishing Environment

Did you know you can actually create a work environment to boost your brain power? "Unfortunately, many people take the wrong approach when decorating their home offices," says Michael J. Gelb, founder of High Performance Learning, Inc. "They create the same dull, stark environment that's been stifling corporate creativity for years." Gelb suggests replacing fluorescent lights with halogen, incandescent, or natural light. He also swears by his hammock and the ten-minute brain breaks he takes regularly.

Gelb has created what he calls a "brain-nourishing environment" in his Great Falls, Virginia, home office, which he shares with his wife. "I have a large dry-erase board and scores of magic markers for mapping out projects or things to do. I've realized that the mind remembers in images, not words, so I create drawings of anything I need to recall."

Gelb's office is filled with flowers, plants, books, stimulating artwork, colorful carpeting, decorator accents, and even a set of juggling balls. "Nothing balances the brain like juggling," he insists. His window offers a picturesque view of a wooded area and he fills the air with classical music. "Everywhere I look, I see something that inspires and energizes me," says Gelb.

Even so, Gelb's great ideas don't always come when sitting in his office. "Like most people, I get my best ideas when I'm not trying too hard. The trick is to write them down immediately so they're not lost." To that end, Gelb stocks notebooks and microcassette recorders where his best ideas usually strike: by his bedside, in the car, and yes, in the bathroom.

Top Ten Idea-Generating Opportunities

According to research conducted by Chic Thompson, the top ten idea-generating times are when you are:
1. Using the restroom.
2. Showering or shaving. (I read somewhere that Albert Einstein said: "Make friends with your shower. If inspired to sing, maybe the song has an idea in it for you.")
3. Commuting to work.
4. Falling asleep or waking up.
5. In a boring meeting.
6. Reading at leisure.
7. Exercising.
8. Waking in the middle of the night.
9. Listening to a sermon in church.
10. Performing manual labor.

Getting a Fresh Perspective

Dr. Yoshiro NakaMats, inventor of the floppy disk and owner of 2,300 patents (more than double the number held by Thomas Edison), comes up with his best ideas while swimming. "I have a special way of holding my breath and swimming underwater—that's when I come up with my best ideas. I've created a Plexiglas writing pad so that I can stay underwater and record these ideas."

You may never invent anything comparable to the floppy disk, but most people do find that physical exercise, getting out into nature, or even a simple change of venue can get the creative juices flowing.

NakaMats has also designed two rooms in his Tokyo home where he goes for inspiration. His "static room" is a place of peace and quiet. "I keep only natural things in there: a rock garden, natural running water, plants, a five-ton boulder from Kyoto," he says. "I go into the room to free-associate." His "dynamic room" is dark, with black-and-white striped walls, leather furniture, and special audio and video equipment. He begins by listening to jazz and always ends with Beethoven's Fifth Symphony.

As a husband and wife team, you can conduct two-phased, idea-generating sessions. First, generate as many ideas as you can, relying heavily on the more creative partner. Then analyze your ideas to determine which have the most merit. During this phase, give added weight to the insights generated by the more analytical partner.

It Won't Fly If You Don't Try

Whether you have a fleeting notion or a product concept you just can't shake, you'll never know whether it's a great idea or a fluke until you put it out for all the world to see. As Alex Osborn has said, "A fair idea put to use is much better than a great idea kept on the polishing wheel." Don't rest on your laurels. Don't get trapped by what you've always done or how you've always done it. Give each other the freedom to offer up zany ideas in an atmosphere of complete acceptance. Plunge boldly into the arena of ideas and you just might come out a winner.

Idea-Generating Tools

Software.

IdeaFisher consists of two massive databases, QBank and IdeaBank. QBank contains six thousand suggestions and questions designed to help you define a problem or project. After you select a general category, QBank leads you through a series of questions designed to progressively narrow your focus. IdeaBank does the opposite. It contains more than sixty-one thousand words and phrases, arranged by subject, to help you free-associate and spark new ideas. Working together, the QBank and IdeaBank help you generate innovative solutions. A pop-up notepad lets you keep track of your thoughts as you work through the problems. Contact IdeaFisher Systems at 800–289–4332.

Idea Generator is based on Gerard Nierenberg's book *The Art of Creative Thinking*, which is bundled with the program. Idea Generator uses a structured approach to creative problem solving. The program offers seven idea-generating techniques, such as adopting Other Perspectives or deliberately Reversing Your Goals. The program's strength lies in allowing you to look at a problem from many different perspectives. It also helps you break down problems into smaller, more manageable units. It is especially helpful for refining ideas. Contact Experience in Software at 800–678–7008.

Inspiration can best be described as computerized mindmapping. It uses a graphic diagramming environment to create and modify outlines, flow charts, and presentations visuals that can be easily converted into flexible outlines and formal documents. The program includes several templates and samples to get you started. Unlike other programs that prompt you with associations, Inspiration is a tool that lets you quickly jot down disassociated ideas and then go back to establish logical links.

Audiocassettes.

Mindmapping: How to Liberate Your Natural Genius by Michael J. Gelb. This four-cassette series explains the working of the human mind, proposes where ideas come from, and offers step-by-step instructions for generating ideas with the mindmapping technique. Contact Nightengale-Conant at 800–525–9000.

Organizations.

Innovative Thinking Network (ITN). ITN is a forum for sharing information and ideas with peers nationwide. It publishes a bimonthly newsletter offering idea-generating techniques, book reviews, and success stories. ITN holds an annual winter conference and on-line brainstorming sessions. Contact ITN at 1103 Harbor Hills Drive, Santa Barbara, CA 93109.

Creative Education Foundation. Founded by Alex Osborn in 1905, this nonprofit organization promotes creativity and innovative approaches to problem solving. It publishes a quarterly *Journal of Creative Behavior* and a monthly newsletter, *Creativity in Action.* In recent years, their annual conference has attracted over seven hundred attendees from thirty different countries. CEF also offers a forty-eight page Catalog of Creative Resources, including dozens of books and tapes designed to boost your idea power. Contact the Creative Education Foundation at 800–447–2774.

On-line.

Ideas, Inventions, & Innovation Forum (On CompuServe, type: GO INNOVATION). This program offers an entire forum devoted to sharing ideas and updates on the latest innovations in a broad range of fields.

An ample library section records prior on-line brainstorming sessions, product and books reviews, and member announcements.

For Reflection and Discussion

1. Conduct a brain-storming session using the technique described in this chapter. You can start by identifying a specific problem you need to solve or try to generate a fresh idea for a new product or service. Note the results of your brainstorming below.

_____

_____

_____

_____

_____

2. Breaking through mental blocks. If you are bogged down in a problem and need a boost, begin scribbling with a pencil or pick up a small object with your non-dominant hand. The unfamiliar muscular movements from the subordinate side of your body will trigger an electrical flow in the non-dominant side of your brain. The net result? New connections, a new perspective, and possibly a new idea.

PART FIVE

FAMILY MATTERS

15

Keeping Your Business and Personal Lives Separate

KEEPING BUSINESS AND PERSONAL lives separate is a challenge for any couple who works together, but we haven't found many couples with a tougher challenge than Mark and Donna DeLucia, who operate Bucks County Racquet Club. Donna's parents founded the club twenty-five years ago and built their home on the second floor. When they retired a few years back, Donna and her husband moved into the home/club. Their business is literally "under their feet" twenty-four hours a day, seven days a week.

The couple now has ten employees, several of whom previously worked for Donna's parents—who, by the way, had a very different management philosophy. "When we took over, I wrote a memo to the employees," recalls Donna. "I was nice, but firm about the fact that we are a young family and need our privacy. My parents had allowed much more invasion of their personal life than we were willing to allow. Under my parents' management, employees were permitted to come upstairs to the house. Anytime they needed or wanted my parents, they could just knock on the door. There was also a buzzer at the front desk that rang upstairs in the house; it was loud enough to wake the dead."

Donna and Mark instituted crucial changes right away to shield their personal lives. For example, Donna emphasized that her working hours are 9:00 A.M. to 5:00 P.M., Monday through Friday, even though the club is open seven days a week from 8:00 A.M. to 11:00 P.M. "We were not willing to remain on call around the clock. When we are off-duty, we do not expect to be disturbed. Whatever it is, it can keep till morning," says Donna. Then she adds, "Unless, of course, someone is robbing the club or the place is burning down. But those are the only two exceptions to the no-interrupt rule.

"We never, never, never allow our employees to come into our home. Rather than knocking on our door, we have asked them to telephone us, just as they would if we didn't live upstairs. And that awful buzzer hasn't made a peep since the day we took over!"

Donna and Mark close the racquet club entirely during the summer. "We continue to get a lot of phone calls, but we let the answering machine take them. Then we set aside time to return the calls. The key is, we don't let the calls control us; we control the calls."

Donna and Mark try to forget about work when they walk up the stairs each evening. Sometimes that's difficult because customers can get pretty "rowdy" down in the lounge area. The DeLucias have worked extra hard to create a homey living environment. "We completely remodeled the place so it doesn't look like my parents house anymore; now it's really *our house, our hideaway.* We have a fabulous stereo system and we listen to all kinds of music, from classical to jazz and everything in between." Donna also plays keyboard and sings. All that music helps drown out the constant audio reminders of their business downstairs. Most of all, though, the DeLucias say their daughter, Nina, constantly reminds them how important it is to cultivate their family life together.

Distinct Work Area

For couples who work at home like the DeLucias, it is extremely important to establish a distinct work area. Many people make the mistake of having a roving home office. One day they work at the kitchen table; another day they work in the bedroom, or who knows where. Unfortunately, if you work everywhere in your house, then there is no place left to go for refuge. Every room and every piece of furniture holds memories of you slaving over the business. Save your work for regular office hours and always conduct it in one specific place.

Donna's (Partow) first home office was a three-foot by five-foot closet—just large enough to fit in a small desk and chair. It never would have made it onto the cover of *Office Beautiful*, but it served its purpose well. It established a distinct work area and, in many ways, was more efficient than the large office loft we now have. Why? Because Donna only went in there when she was serious about getting work done. When we bought our current home, Donna moved her office into a large loft with huge windows on two sides. It really *looked* like the ultimate home office. Unfortunately, with the beautiful loft setting, it's tempting just to sit and stare at the mountains or city lights in the distance.

The point is, your home office doesn't have to be perfect; it just has to be distinct from the rest of your house. The key is an environment which helps you make the mental shift from your personal life as a mom, dad, spouse, to your business life as an accountant, marketing executive, or whatever. Anything you can do to keep the two domains from merging will ultimately strengthen you in both areas.

Closed Doors

Another important advantage of working in one, and only one, location in your home is that you can close the door when the workday is done. This enables you to make the mental shift back to your role as wife/mother or husband/father. An open office door is a constant invitation to work. If you heed that invitation too often, you won't have a personal life worth preserving.

Here again, we have found that our loft (which seemed so idyllic in the model home) is extremely ineffective. Every time we walk by, we see the mounds of work waiting to be done. If at all possible, set up an office with a closeable door. Alternatively, you can create a partition with bookshelves, a privacy screen, or a sturdy piece of fabric. Shortly after we wrote this, we decided to move our office out of the illustrious loft and into the lowly guest room over the garage. Now we'll never make it into *Office Beautiful* magazine, but we're much more productive!

Set Specific Working Hours

We think the DeLucias had a good policy. You need to establish specific hours for working and specific hours for *not* working. Most self-employed people tend to drift to one of two extremes: procrastination or workaholism. Either they never get around to work, in which case they urgently need to set aside *office* time and stick to it, or they work day and night, in which case they definitely need to set aside *personal* time and stick to it.

Many people find dressing professionally makes a big difference. They shower, shave, get dressed to the tie (or right down to stockings and pumps, as the case may be) each day prior to reporting to their home office. They insist this makes it easier to shift gears from personal to professional life. At the end of the day, they change back into their casual clothes and mentally switch gears into the personal mode.

We actually knew a man who got dressed, picked up his briefcase, walked around the block, and reentered his home office by a separate door. At the end of the day, he reversed the process and came home through the front door. This little ritual helped him make the mental shift. It may sound silly (looks pretty silly, too), but it works!

Use a Work Log

An excellent way to get a handle on whether you or your spouse are working too much or too little is to maintain a work log. Every time you get down to work, sign in the date and time. When you walk away—even if it's just to go down to the kitchen for a "quick" snack— sign out. If one of you struggles with procrastination, perhaps you can keep the log on your desk and indicate *specifically* what work you accomplish. It's quite possible to sit in your office eighteen hours a day, but only *work* three hours. (This, of course, is a highly refined art. If you need instructions, contact Donna; she's the expert.)

In this situation you are never really free. When you are in the office, you're not free because you know you should be productive and you're not. Nothing is more draining than arriving at the end of the day having accomplished nothing. Meanwhile, you've put your personal life on hold while you sit in your office dawdling. Yet you feel guilty taking personal time when you know you accomplished nothing during your so-called working hours. (We told you this was a fine art!)

The only cure is to discipline yourself to *actually* work during working hours and to *only* work during working hours. Then, when you walk away from work, walk away completely. Log out, close the door, and go enjoy life. Both your personal life and your business will profit in the end.

Get a Separate Phone or Distinctive Ring

You will also need to distinguish between business and personal phone calls so you can ignore business calls during nonworking hours. One option, of course, is to purchase a separate business line, complete with voice messaging or answering machine to take calls when you are unavailable. We use the more affordable "distinctive ringing" service offered by our local phone company. We have two phone numbers, but one phone line. A normal ring indicates a personal phone call; a double ring indicates a business call. If a call comes in during an unusual time, we have the option of letting it go to voice mail and dealing with it when we're "back in the office."

Take Weekends Off

If at all possible, don't work on weekends. At least take Sunday as a day of rest—even God did, and running the universe is more important than whatever business you're in! Suzanne Shell of Tumbleweed Upholstery reports, "Our Sunday-off rule is about the best decision we've ever made. We come back to the shop refreshed and ready to face another week." All work and no recreation is a formula many couples have used to destroy their marriages. It's not a pattern we want to repeat. How about you?

If you work at home during the week, get away from the house on weekends. Go hiking, biking, visiting friends, or whatever. Don't let home sweet home become prison sour prison.

Bill and Diane Black, of Beyond Words, say, "We like to take our family on weekend trips to nearby attractions or to visit out-of-town family. That forces us to have a life outside of work and gives us additional topics and shared memories to talk about. We have a deep appreciation for the term 'getting out of the house.' Once a year, we attend an annual convention for one of the organizations we work with. We build in several days before the convention to travel—without the children—so we can relax and recharge."

191

"We've found we need an escape," say Perry and Gail Hayden, who've been married for thirty years and worked together for seventeen. "At present, outdoor physical activities, like mountain biking, offer the most effective escape. We are forever trying different things to make the most of our time off. We never go to the same place twice, so after thirty years of vacationing we've got quite a storehouse of interesting memories to ponder. We eat out a lot at a variety of restaurants. We are always trying to explore new adventures. I think it has been one of the keys to keeping our marriage alive and keeping us satisfied with life." Yet even the Haydens admit "carving out a personal life is the most difficult part of being in business together."

Keep Personal Disagreements Out of the Office and Business Conflicts Out of the Bedroom

When you've had one of *those* mornings, it's hard to leave the conflict behind when you report to the office (home or elsewhere). It's equally hard to battle over the business all day and then return home to play the role of honeymooners. We are all human. It's impossible to completely divorce what we do from who we are. It's inevitable that any business criticisms you make of your spouse may carry over into your private time, and vice versa.

As always, your best defense is a good offense; implement as many of the suggestions in this chapter as possible. Try to deal with work-related issues during working hours and save personal discussions for your private hours. We know it's much easier said than done. The point is, be on guard to the potential pitfalls of completely submerging your personal life into your business life.

For Reflection and Discussion

Indicate which of the following policies you plan to implement to keep your business and personal life separate:

Distinct Work Area

_____

_____

Closed Door Policy

_____

_____

Specific Working Hours

_____

_____

Work Log

_____

_____

Separate Phone Line

_____

_____

Weekends Off

_____

_____

Keep Personal Disagreements at Home

_____

_____

Keep Business Conflicts at the Office

_____

_____

16
What About Young Children?

JIM AND JILL MAPSTEAD, whom you met back in Chapter 12, have worked hard to create an incredibly nurturing environment for their two daughters, four-and-a-half-year-old Jesse and four-month-old Leah. As a result, Jesse plays quietly in her bedroom each morning for several hours so Mom can work at home. Of course, Jesse is not playing in an ordinary room! Her headboard is a gigantic cut-out cloud. The back wall is painted royal blue and has a big cut-out moon and stars. That's the nighttime wall. Together, Jill and Jesse created a daytime wall by sponge-painting it light blue and white. Then Jim cut out and mounted wooden clouds. The window even has a cloud-shaped curtain.

All of the walls are covered with removable abstract stickers, made by 3M, so Jesse can redecorate her room anytime she likes. She has a Japanese futon for her dolls, a large bean bag chair, and a shelf bursting with great books. Since Mom and Dad have read them all aloud, Jesse can sit and "read" them to herself.

The Mapsteads removed the door from the large closet and filled it with space organizers and shelf units, which Jim bought at Home Depot. One area is filled with building blocks, marble towers, and tinker toys. Another shelf holds board games. There's an entire Art Center with lots of messy things to do. Of course, there's also a little mat and apron that Jesse has been taught to use. Jill has actually taught Jesse to enjoy playing "clean-up," with Mom acting as Mr. Inspector. Sometimes they have races to see who can put things away faster.

The Moral of the Story

Okay, what's all this talk about clouds and sponge-painting? Jill sums it up best: "We put in the effort up-front and now we're reaping the benefits." Whether you have one child or five; whether you have toddlers or teenagers, the secret to your survival and theirs is *advance planning*. If you don't develop specific strategies to ensure the well-being of your children, they may end up neglected and embittered. And no one can call himself successful if his children call him a failure.

Donna has written two other books, which women in particular will find very helpful. First, *Homemade Business: A Woman's Step-by-Step Guide to Earning Money at Home* (Focus on the Family, 1992) includes twenty chapters on successfully running a business from home. There are also two chapters that specifically cover managing your children. (To obtain a copy, visit your local Christian bookstore or call 800-A-FAMILY.) Second, check out *No More Lone Ranger Moms* (Bethany House, 1995). It will arm you with an effective battle plan for networking with other women to find the support you need to balance family and career. Again, try a local Christian bookstore or call 800-328-6109. Following are just a few of the ideas found in *Homemade Business* and *No More Lone Ranger Moms*:

Baby-Sitting Co-op

Rather than rely on the capitalist instincts of strangers (i.e., baby-sitters-for-hire), why not form a cooperative of like-minded mothers to exchange free baby-sitting. The simplest way to do this is by using a coupon system. For a small entry fee, each woman receives a number (about 20) of laminated coupons worth one-half hour each. Compile a typed list with the names, addresses, and phone numbers of participants and you're off. (Well, there's a bit more to it than that, but you'll have to read *No More Lone Ranger Moms* to find out!)

You can also use a more informal method. For several months, Donna and another mother in the neighborhood exchanged children one full day per week. Those long stretches of time, knowing Leah was receiving excellent care from a mom who shared our values, were used by Donna to write much of this book. You'll be amazed how much you can accomplish with the help of your baby-sitting co-op.

Playgroups

Another marvelous tool is a parent-led playgroup. We have six mothers who take turns leading our playgroup. Each week, all the children (four- and five-year-old girls only) meet at the sponsoring mother's home. It is her responsibility to plan fun activities for two and a half hours. Meanwhile, the other five mothers are free to use the time as they please. It's convenient, because we all live within a few blocks of each other. We trust one another implicitly and our girls love this special time together. Again, you will find much more information on organizing a playgroup in *No More Lone Ranger Moms*.

Videos

Cameron thinks Donna is too strict on this subject, but Leah is not permitted to watch any television other than the children's shows on Public Television. We encourage Barney, and the others are just okay. However, she has quite a video collection and can watch them whenever she likes. All videos are carefully screened for educational and/or literary value, so we actually feel good about her watching them. Using the VCR as a baby-sitter is a tricky business, to be sure. However, if used intelligently and within reason, we think the VCR is an acceptable way to create some work time for Mom.

CD-ROM

Our neighbor recently bought a CD-ROM drive for their computer, which came with a load of educational software. We spent several hours watching Leah interact with the system and we were very impressed. This looks like a great way to productively occupy children from four years old and up.

Parents' Helper

Here's one of our favorite options for getting work done while making sure Leah receives the attention she needs. Since she was an infant, we have hired young girls in our neighborhood to come over after school and play with Leah. The girls are delighted with an opportunity to make extra money, Leah has adored all of these young girls, and Donna has been able to work at home effectively.

The beauty of this set-up is that at least one parent is at home, so if any problems develop, he or she is available to handle them. You can work in peace knowing your child is just fine. Lingering doubts in the minds of many parents about the care of their children can sap their productivity.

In addition, a parent's helper has only one job: caring for your child or children. Her attention is not divided between twenty different kids. Some especially well-trained young girls will be able to enrich your child's life immensely. Our current helper is Jill Dueck, a delightful young girl who arrives with a bag full of fun and educational things to do with Leah. Since she attends home school, she is able to come at 1:00 P.M. on weekdays.

You can also use parents' helpers (both boys and girls) for cleaning, running errands, doing odd jobs. We have had boys mow the lawn and do yardwork, while girls have helped with cooking, cleaning, and other household projects. We are biased, of course, but we find that home-schooled children are generally more responsible than most other young people. More importantly, they have more free time and more flexibility. If you are looking for a parents' helper, contact your local home-school support group. Perhaps they can put you in touch with some job candidates.

Parks

Depending upon the nature of your work, what part of the country you live in, and how close the nearest park is, making use of the local park facilities can be an excellent work strategy. We are fortunate enough to live in Arizona, where the weather is beautiful nine months of the year. Donna frequently takes Leah to the park (a mile from our home) in the afternoons. Leah enjoys the fresh air and swings, while Donna works on her latest writing projects. The change of scenery does both of them a lot of good.

Designated Toys and Play Areas

While researching *Homemade Business*, Donna interviewed many work-at-home moms who had set up a specific area in their home with special toys that could only be played with while Mommy worked. We love the way the Mapsteads, the couple at the beginning of this chapter, have created such a wonderful environment for their daughter. We think taking care of the children's business before trying to attend to your own is a great strategy.

Preschool

For children over three years of age, preschool is an option many parents choose. A number of mothers swear by it, so if it's right for you, you can carve out some quiet time to pursue your business. We tried a co-operative preschool at a local church, but it wasn't right for us. We noticed that when Leah spent the morning in a room with twenty other kids, she acted crazy the rest of the day. Besides, by the time Donna dragged Leah out of bed (neither of them is a morning person), got her dressed, fed, and out the door to preschool, then drove home and got down to work, it was time to get back in the car to pick up Leah. It just wasn't worth it.

Hired Baby-sitters

Yes, this is an option, though we don't like it much. We are contrasting "hired baby-sitters" with your mom, your sister, your neighbor, or your best friend. We're referring to leaving your child(ren) in the hands of someone who advertises "Loving Care" with flyers tacked to telephone poles. There was a time, when Leah was very young, when we had no support system of any kind and finances were desperate. Donna was forced to leave Leah with hired baby-sitters when she went out on sales calls for her commercial copywriting business. Every time, she was terrified that Leah was not receiving proper care. Even several years later, Donna occasionally wakes up at night, wondering if any of these strangers hurt our child when we weren't there to protect her.

We really *do* understand that sometimes finances

and circumstances are such that you have no other choice. *We have been there!* We want to encourage you, though, to use maximum creativity when arranging for the care of your young children. Start a playgroup; join a baby-sitting co-op; find a parents' helper. Talk your parents into moving closer to your home. (Don't laugh, the Mapsteads did it and they are so happy they did! There's just no substitute for Grandma.)

Yes, you can balance your family and your business. It takes hard work and creativity. But it's well worth the effort.

For Reflection and Discussion

Following is a list of the strategies found in this chapter. After each one that appeals to you, jot down some action steps you can take to begin implementing it.

Baby-sitting Co-op

_____

_____

Playgroup

_____

_____

Videos

_____

_____

CD-ROMs

_____

_____

Parents' Helper

_____

_____

Parks

_____

Play Area

Preschool

Hired Baby-sitter

17
Involving Your Children in Your Business

MANY OF THE COUPLES we interviewed had involved their children in their business in some way, at some time or another. Two of the most long-term business relationships existed for the Rhodes and the Haydens. Jim and Naomi Rhode, of SmartPractice, have three married children and nine incredibly beautiful and unbelievably smart grandchildren. (Naomi, we hope we got that right.) "Starting from the time our oldest was thirteen, all three children traveled with us every summer for fifteen years. We conducted family-oriented seminars, so it was only natural for them to come along. Our kids developed their own presentations for the children and teenagers while we presented our seminars for the parents. It worked beautifully." Today, their son-in-law is Executive Vice-President of SmartPractice and their daughter works for them on a consulting basis.

Perry and Gayle Hayden say both of their children have always been involved in the business. "Our daughter, Wendy, who is now twenty-six, works for us full-time. When she was twelve years old, she started working with Gayle at craft fairs helping "man" the booth. When she reached adulthood, she worked elsewhere for six years before returning to the family business. Our son David is now in college full-time, but over the years he has also been active in the business."

PROS

Let's take a quick look at the advantages of involving your children in the family business:

1. *Teaches responsibility.* Your children will acquire a very rare commodity in today's society: a sense of responsibility.

2. *They are safe.* When your children are working with you, they are safe. At least you know where they are!

3. *Teaches work skills, good habits, and good values.* We consider this the greatest advantage of involving Leah in the business. We want to teach her, from a very young age, to develop a proper attitude and respect for work.

4. *Informed career choice.* Your children may very well grow up and decide they *don't* want to follow in your career steps. That's okay. At least they'll have a good idea of what they don't want to do. And along the way, they'll probably develop a much clearer sense of what career they would like to pursue.

5. *Avoids the Catch 22.* You can't get a job without experience and you can't get experience without a job. When your children go out into that great big scary world of job-hunting, at least they'll have something to show for their first eighteen years on the planet. Potential employers are bound to give the edge to a teen who has been working in the family business since he was four, over the teen who has spent his summers at the beach.

6. *Provides time together.* By including your children in your business, you automatically increase the amount of time you spend together. Of course, the QUALITY of that time will depend largely on you—how

you conduct your business and how you have raised your children.

7. *It's cheap labor.* Okay, we admit it. We really like this advantage. In the old days, people had twelve kids just to help run the farm. Maybe they had a good thing going, after all. Now, if only we could give birth to a graphic designer, an audio-visual specialist, a publicist, and a seminar promoter, the Partows would have it made!

8. *Flexible resource.* Unlike most employees, your children will probably cheer when you tell them there's not enough work to keep them busy for the next month. You can also increase hours when needed, as long as you do so within reason and within state laws.

9. *On-the-job training for your successors.* Now remember, Mom and Dad, there's no guarantee that Junior will want to take over the family business. Please, please, don't force your children to follow in your footsteps if it's not the right path for them. However, let's assume Junior wants to run the business someday. The many years of working alongside you will leave him (or her) in good standing to take over the business when you are ready to retire.

CONS

1. *They may grow to resent the business and you.* Yes, it's true. Your beloved business may become a curse to your beloved children. Especially if you treat your beloved business as though it were *more important* than your children. This is easy to do, and we know quite a few adults who want nothing to do with their parents or their parents' business. Why? Because they resent having played second fiddle to a balance sheet, and we don't blame them.

2. *May be overworked.* In the previous section we touted the joys of a flexible workforce, but be careful not to overwork your children. It's not right and, again, they

will come to resent both you and the business.

3. *It's expensive if you simply make up work for them to do.* Some of you may have worked for a company where the owner's children made little contribution, but drew a hefty paycheck anyway. This "free-ride" syndrome is a trap for children, both young and old. Remember, you do your children no favor by teaching them the world will give them something for nothing.

4. *Undue pressure to follow in the family business.* Surely we all know someone who has been put in this situation—it is not enviable. Again, the key is letting your children develop their own natural talents and interests. If those fit in with the future of your business, wonderful. Let them join if they wish. But if your son wants to play the violin and you run an autobody shop, don't make him skip music lessons to repaint fenders.

5. *Potential customer-relations and employee-relations problems.* Even hard-working children of the boss often get a bum rap, from both customers and fellow employees. Some people may secretly envy them, thinking they are getting an unfair advantage. As a result, employing your children can be a breeding ground for resentment and conflict. If someone unjustly attacks your children, cut them off and do it quickly. On the other hand, if *everyone* criticizes your children, maybe it's time to dish up some tough love.

Tips From Parents Who Employ Their Children

If you do decide to hire your children, keep in mind the following tips offered by parents we interviewed:

1. Make sure your son or daughter is well-suited to the business. Understand his or her temperament, talents, and interests.

2. Find the right role. Help him find a place where he can successfully contribute to the company's future.

3. Assign age-appropriate tasks to younger children.

There's a big difference between what preteens, teens, and adults can do. Set realistic expectations according to their age group. If you aren't sure what's realistic, talk to other parents and business owners to get a better idea.

4. Compensation Strategies. There are a variety of ways to compensate your children. Here's an overview:

Hourly Wage—Obviously, this is the only appropriate method for paying an adult child. You can also pay children and teens an hourly wage.

Allowance—If your business is based at home, you can require your children to fulfill certain duties as part of their overall chores. In return, they receive a fixed weekly allowance.

Volunteer—This is for you big meanies out there! Yes, we did interview some folks who expected their children to work for the family business *because it was the family business*. Since the business puts food on the table and the children like to eat, they should be willing to work. We think this is a bit cruel . . . but, it's an option!

Tax Implications. Go ahead and put your kids on the payroll. Since they are in a lower tax bracket, it is a perfectly legitimate way to save on your taxes. However, once your children turn eighteen, they are taxed at the same rate as the rest of us.

Love Them, Either Way

Whether or not you decide to employ your children, remember to love them, and not just in words. Love them enough to keep them first and foremost in your lives. Love them enough to let them become all God intended them to be. Love them enough to let them choose their own path, even if it strays far from *your* dreams. A family business can be a wonderful experience or it can be a horrible one. The priorities you set and keep will make the difference for your children.

For Reflection and Discussion

1. Which of the PROS are most significant for you and why?
Mention as many as you like:

_____

_____

_____

_____

_____

2. Which of the CONS are of most significance to you? How
will you guard against them?

_____

_____

_____

_____

_____

18
Final Thoughts

WHEN WE UNDERTOOK the project of writing this book about working with the one you love, our goal was to encourage and inspire other couples. We felt we'd discovered a better way of life than that of hopping subway cars and heading in two different directions each morning. We hope throughout the pages of this book we have fulfilled our mission: that you have, indeed, caught the exciting vision of working together as husband and wife. We trust you learned a thing or two about business management and about handling the unique challenges that a joint business presents to your marriage relationship. But, most of all, we want you to walk away from these pages with fresh enthusiasm. Because, in the end, it is your enthusiasm that will carry the day.

Henry Ford said, "You can do anything if you have enthusiasm. Enthusiasm is the yeast that makes your hopes rise to the stars. Enthusiasm is the spark in your eye, the swing in your gait, the grip of your hand, the irresistible surge of your will and your energy to execute ideas. Enthusiasts are fighters, they have fortitude, they have staying qualities. Enthusiasm is at the bottom of all progress. With it, there is accomplishment. Without it, there are only alibis."[1]

[1] Quotes on Line: "Words from the Wise," by Keith D. Mohler. AskSam Software, 1992.

As we talked with dozens of entrepreneurial couples from around the country—by phone, fax, mail, and e-mail—we had many encouraging and inspiring conversations. We set out to encourage others and ended up wildly encouraged ourselves! Our hopes, indeed, rose to the stars. We noticed a brighter spark in each other's eyes and even that livelier gait that Ford described! When we grew weary in the task, the exciting reports we heard propelled us forward. They gave us that irresistible surge of will and energy to finish this book, even though it often meant working into the small hours of the morning.

We'd like to share with you some of the wisdom gleaned from the many couples we interviewed. We asked each couple to list some Do's and Don'ts to share with our readers. Here, in their own words, are some of their insights:

A Collection of Do's and Don'ts From the Pros

DO remember this is a business. Even if it is a family affair, your livelihood depends on your professionalism and the quality of the product you produce.

DO respect your spouse's strengths and weaknesses.

DO respect the other's area of expertise.

DO share the dirty jobs . . . and the fun jobs, too.

DO remember that sometimes your spouse will have a bad day. Be willing to cover for him or her and pick up the slack. Your partner will return the favor when you need it.

DO present a united front to employees, vendors, and customers.

DO remember your spouse isn't the family dog. He or she can recognize mistakes without having his or her nose rubbed into it.

DO remember common courtesies such as "Please" and "Thank you." Marriage is no excuse for rudeness.

DO remember to compliment each other for a job well done.

DO make judicious use of your answering machine or voice mail system.

DO trust each other completely.

DO clarify who is in charge of what.

DO go out to lunch or dinner alone at least once a week. It doesn't have to be fancy, but you do have to go alone.

DO respect the other's workstyle. It may be radically different from your own.

DO actively cultivate your sense of humor.

DON'T expect your spouse to read your mind. Say what you need.

DON'T come behind the other person and second-guess his or her decisions.

DON'T take professional criticism personally. This is business.

DON'T expect more than your spouse can give.

DON'T contradict your spouse behind his or her back.

DON'T bad-mouth your spouse to a customer.

DON'T make your spouse's job more difficult. Do what you are supposed to do, even if you don't like doing it.

DON'T call each other names or make cruel remarks.

DON'T let jealousy creep into your marriage or your business.

DON'T duplicate efforts.

Well, those are some good thoughts to leave you with. In closing, we'd like to share a poem we have posted on the wall of our home office. May it inspire and guide you as it has us:

> Finish every day and be done with it.
> You have done what you could.
> Some blunders and absurdities no doubt crept in;
> forget them as soon as you can.

Tomorrow is a new day;
begin it well and serenely
and with too high a spirit to be cumbered
by your old nonsense.
This day is all that is good and fair.
It is too dear, with its hopes and invitations,
to waste a moment on yesterdays.
                                        —Emerson

An exciting tomorrow awaits you as you journey together as partners in love and in business. Savor each day and each moment you have to enjoy the privilege of working with the one you love.

19
Help Is On the Way: Resource Listing

ASSOCIATIONS

American Association for Medical Transcription
P.O. Box 576187
Modesto, CA 95357
800–982–2182

American Association of Exporters & Importers
11 West 42nd Street, 30th floor
New York, NY 10036
212–944–2230

American Business Women's Association
9100 Ward Parkway
P.O. Box 8728
Kansas City, MO 64114–0728

American Institute of CPAs
1211 Avenue of the Americas
New York, NY 10036
212–575–6200

American Society of Interior Designers
608 Massachusetts Avenue NE
Washington, DC 20002
202–546–3480

American Society of Journalists and Authors, Inc.
1501 Broadway, Suite 302
New York, NY 10036
212–997–0947

American Society of Travel Agents
1101 King Street
Alexandria, VA 22314
703–892–1500

Association of Independent Information Professionals
3724 FM 1960 West, Suite 214
Houston, TX 77068
713–537–9051

Association of Management Consultant Firms
230 Park Avenue, Suite 544
New York, NY 10169
212–697–9693

Center for Family Business
7000 Bianca Avenue
Van Nuys, CA 91411
216–442–0800

Direct Marketing Association
11 West 42nd Street
New York, NY 10036–8096
212–768–7277

Direct Selling Association
1776 K Street, NW
Suite 600
Washington, DC 20006
202–293–5760

Federation of Small Business
407 S. Dearborn, Suite 500
Chicago, IL 60605
312–427–0206

Graphic Artists Guild
11 West 20th Street, 8th floor
New York, NY 10011–3704
212–463–7730

Independent Computer Consultants Association
933 Gardenview Office Parkway
St. Louis, MO 63141
800–438–4222
314–997–4633

Information Industry Association
555 New Jersey Avenue NW
Suite 800
Washington, DC 20001
202–639–8262

International Association for Financial Planning
2 Concourse Parkway
Suite 800
Atlanta, GA 30328
404–395–1605 / 800–945–IAFP

International Council for Small Business
3674 Lindell Boulevard
St. Louis, MO 63108
314–658–3850

International Franchise Association
1350 New York Avenue NW
Washington, DC 20005
202–628–8000

National Association of Secretarial Services
3637 Fourth Street North, Suite 330
St. Petersburg, FL 33704
813–823–3646

National Association of Women Business Owners
600 S. Federal Street
Suite 400
Chicago, IL 60605
312–922–0465

National Speakers Association
1500 S. Priest Drive
Tempe, AZ 85281
602–968–0911

Professional Photographers of America
1090 Executive Way
Des Plaines, IL 60018
708–299–8161

Video Retailers Association
2455 East Sunrise Boulevard
Ft. Lauderdale, FL 33304–1877
305–561–3505

GOVERNMENT

Copyright Office
Library of Congress
Washington, DC 20559
Information line:
202–707–3000

Export-Import Bank
811 Vermont Avenue NW
Washington, DC 20571
202–566–8990

Internal Revenue Service
Tax Help Line:
800–829–1040

Service Corps of Retired Executives (SCORE)
To find the office nearest you,
call 800–827–5722.

TAX PAMPHLETS

The IRS has a series of free tax publications available by calling
800-TAX-FORM (800–829–3676).

Guide #	Publication Name
334	Tax Guide for Small business
463	Travel, Entertainment, and Gift Expenses
505	Tax Withholding and Estimated Tax
508	Taxable and Non-Taxable Income
529	Miscellaneous Deductions
533	Self-Employment Tax
535	Business Expenses
538	Accounting Periods and Methods
541	Tax Information on Partnerships
542	Tax Information on Corporations
560	Retirement Plans for the Self-Employed
583	Taxpayers Starting a Business
587	Business Use of Your Home
589	Tax Information on S Corporations
590	Individual Retirement Arrangements
917	Business Use of a Car
937	Business Reporting
946	How to Begin Depreciating Your Property

MAGAZINES AND OTHER PERIODICALS

Entrepreneur Magazine
2392 Morse Avenue
P.O. Box 19787
Irvine, CA 92714
800–421–2300

Home Office Computing
P.O. Box 51344
Boulder, CO 80321
800–288–7812

Inc.
38 Commercial Wharf
Boston, MA 02110
800–234–0999

Nation's Business
1615 H Street, NW
Washington, DC 20062
800–638–6582

Success: The Magazine for Today's Entrepreneurial Mind
P.O. Box 53140
Harlan, IA 51537
800–234–7324

The Whole Work Catalog
New Careers Center, Inc.
1515 23rd Street
P.O. Box 339
Boulder, CO 80306
303–447–1087

AUDIO AND VIDEO CASSETTES

CareerTrack
3085 Center Green Drive
P.O. Box 18778
Boulder, CO 80308
800–334–1018
Offers professional development and management training via audio and video, in addition to live seminars nationwide.

Nightengale-Conant Corp.
7300 N. Lehigh Avenue
Niles, IL 60714
800–323–5532
Nightingale-Conant offers a wide variety of audio and video training materials geared toward personal achievement, business success, and motivation.

BOOKS

BUSINESS PLANNING

Abrams, Rhonda. *The Successful Business Plan: Secrets & Strategies.* Grants Pass, Ore.: Oasis Press, 1992. (800–228–2275)
Bangs, David H. Jr., *The Business Planning Guide: Creating a Plan for Success in Your Own Business.* Dover, N.H.: Upstart Books, 1993.
McKeever, Mike. *How to Write a Business Plan.* Berkeley, Calif.: Nolo Press, 1993.
Mancuso, Joseph R. *How to Write a Winning Business Plan.* Englewood Cliffs, N.J.: Prentice Hall, 1990.

CHOOSING THE RIGHT BUSINESS

Anderson, Nancy. *Work with Passion: How to Do What You Love for a Living.* San Rafael, Calif.: New World Library, 1993.
Hucknall, Nanette. *Finding Your Work, Loving Your Life.* York Beach, Maine: Samuel Weiser, Inc., 1992.
Sinetar, Marsha. *Do What You Love, the Money Will Follow: Discovering Your Right Livelihood.* Mahwah, N.J.: Paulist Press, 1987.

Zina Bennet, Hal and Susan J. Sparrow. *Follow Your Bliss*. New York: Avon Books, 1990

CUSTOMER SERVICE

LeBoeuf, Michael. *How to Win Customers and Keep Them for Life*. N.Y.: Berkley Books, 1987.

EMPLOYEES

Grensing, Lin. *A Small Business Guide to Employee Selection: Finding, Interviewing and Hiring the Right People*. Bellingham, WA: Self-Counsel Press, 1991.

IDEA GENERATING

Buzan, Tony. *Use Both Sides of Your Brain*. Plume Publishing. (800–526–0275).

De Bono, Edward. *Serious Creativity: Using the Power of Lateral Thinking to Create New Ideas*. HarperBusiness. (800–331–3761).

Goleman, Daniel. *The Creative Spirit*. Plume Publishing. (800–526–0275).

Osborn, Alex. *Your Creative Power*. Motorola University Press.

Thompson, Chic. *What a Great Idea!* HarperCollins. (800–331–3761).

Von Oech, Roger. *A Whack on the Side of the Head*. Warner Books. (800–343–9204).

Wycoff, Joyce. *Mindmapping: Your Personal Guide to Exploring Creativity and Problem-Solving*. Berkley Books, (800–788–6262).

LEGAL AND FINANCIAL ISSUES

Barrett, E. Thorpe. *Write Your Own Business Contracts*. Grants Pass, Ore.: The Oasis Press, 1991.

Bernstein, Peter W., ed. *The Ernst & Young Tax Guide*. New York: John Wiley & Sons. Published annually.

Clifford, Denis and Ralph Warner. *The Partnership Book: How to Write a Partnership Agreement*. Berkeley: Nolo Press, 1991.

Droms, William G. *Finance & Accounting for Non-Financial Managers*. Addison-Wesley. (800–822–6339).

Ellentuck, Albert B. *Leventhol and Horwath Small Business Tax Planning Guide*. Avon Books.

Friedman, Robert. *The Complete Small Business Legal Guide*. Enterprise Dearborn. (800–982–2850).

Sitarz, Daniel. *The Complete Book of Small Business Legal Forms*. Boulder, Colo.: Nova Publishing, 1993.

MANAGEMENT

Silbiger, Steven. *The Ten-Day MBA*. William Morrow. (800–873–9389).

MARKETING AND SALES

Blake, Gary and Robert W. Bly. *How to Promote Your Own Business*. N.Y.: Plume, 1983.

Edwards, Paul and Sarah, with Laura Clampitt Douglas. *Getting Business to Come to You*. Los Angeles, Jeremy P. Tarcher, 1991.
Connor, Dick and Jeff Davidson. *Getting New Clients*. John Wiley & Sons. (800–225–5945).
Hopkins, Tom. *How to Master the Art of Selling*. Warner Books.
Levinson, Jay Conrad. *Guerrilla Marketing*. Boston: Houghton Mifflin, 1984.
Levinson, Jay Conrad. *Guerrilla Marketing Attack*. Houghton Mifflin, 1989.
Levinson. *Guerrilla Marketing Weapons*, 1990
Levinson. *Guerrilla Marketing Excellence*, 1993.
Miller, Robert B. And Stephen E. Heiman. *Strategic Selling*. Miller Heiman. (800–526–6400).
Phillips, Michael and Salli Rasberry. *Marketing Without Advertising*. Berkeley, Calif.: Nolo Press, 1993.
Ries, Al and Jack Trout. *The 22 Immutable Laws of Marketing*. Harper Business. (800–242–7737).
RoAne, Susan. *The Secrets of Savvy Networking*. Warner Books. 800–343–9204.
Slutsky, Jeff. *How to Get Clients*. N.Y.: Warner Books, 1992.
Zigler, Zig. *Secrets of Closing the Sale*, Berkley Books.

TIME MANAGEMENT

Covey, Stephen. *The Seven Habits of Highly Effective People*. N.Y.: Fireside Books, 1990.
Covey, Stephen. *First Things First*. N.Y.: Simon & Schuster, 1994.
Hummel, Charles E. *Tyranny of the Urgent*. InterVarsity Press.
Lakein, Alan. *How to Get Control of Your Time and Your Life*. N.Y.: Signet Books, 1973.
LeBoeuf, Michael. *Working Smart: How to Accomplish More in Half the Time*, McGraw Hill.
Meyer, Jeffrey. *If You Haven't Got Time to Do It Right, When Will You Find the Time to Do It Over?* N.Y.: Fireside Books, 1990.
Waitley, Denis. *Timing Is Everything*. Nashville, Tenn.: Thomas Nelson Publishers, 1992.

TRENDS (WATCHING, ANTICIPATING AND EXPLOITING)

Burrus, Daniel. *Technotrends: How to Use Technology to Go Beyond Your Competition*. N.Y.: Harper Business, 1993.
Celente, Gerald with Tom Milton. *Trend Tracking*. Warner Books. (800–343–9204).
Naisbitt, John and Patricia Aburdene. *Megatrends 2000*. N.Y.: Avon Books, 1990.
Popcorn, Faith. *The Popcorn Report*. N.Y.: Harper Business, 1991.
Toffler, Alvin. *The Third Wave*. N.Y.: Morrow Books, 1980.

WORK-AT-HOME

Cook, Mel. *Home Business, Big Business*. N.Y.: Macmillan Publishing, 1992.

Edwards, Paul and Sarah. *Working From Home.* Los Angeles: Jeremy P. Tarcher, 1990.

Edwards, Paul and Sarah. *The Best Home Business for the 90s.* Los Angeles: Jeremy P. Tarcher, 1991.

Edwards, Paul and Sarah. *Making It on Your Own.* Los Angeles: Jeremy P. Tarcher, 1991.